HOW TO BE
A LANDLORD

HOW TO BE
A LANDLORD

All About Tenant Selection,
Rental Agreements, Money Matters,
and Sharing Your Space

*Gary and Mary
Tondorf-Dick*

DOUBLEDAY & COMPANY, INC.
GARDEN CITY, NEW YORK
1985

This book is not intended to be a substitute for professional legal or financial advice.

Library of Congress Cataloging in Publication Data
Tondorf-Dick, Gary.
    How to be a landlord.
    "A Dolphin book."
    1. Rental housing. 2. Landlord and tenant.
I. Tondorf-Dick, Mary. II. Title.
HD1394.T66   1985   333.5'4'068
ISBN 0-385-27877-2
Library of Congress Catalog Card Number: 84-25906

For Daniel Joseph

Contents

TEMPORARY RESTRAINING ORDER
"SELF-HELP" EVICTIONS
SUMMARY PROCESS

Introduction

With mortgage interest rates at 15 percent, the dream of owning a single-family house or large co-op is fading for the seemingly affluent baby boom professional. Along with interest rates, inflation and the cost of goods and services have kept the cost of housing high. If you buy a one-hundred-thousand-dollar house at 15 percent interest with 20 percent down, you can expect to pay about one thousand dollars per month for principal and interest alone; taxes, heat, maintenance, utilities, insurance and repairs are additional expenses which can bring your total monthly housing costs to sixteen hundred dollars.

As a result, many first-time buyers have found a solution to ease the burden of impossible monthly payments: they are becoming landlords—not of sprawling apartment complexes but of two- or three-unit houses. In cities, a brownstone can provide two rental units; in the suburbs, a split-level ranch or rambling Victorian can provide an apartment or room to rent. For many people, the income generated by the rental units makes the critical difference between renting and affording a home of one's own.

Chances are, if you bought this book, you already own or have just bought a house with one or more rental units. You've probably been coached on the many financial advantages of owning rental property. If you've been a tenant yourself, you probably think you know what makes a good landlord and what pitfalls you want to avoid. But you are probably not familiar with a landlord's problems and headaches; these you took for granted when you were a tenant.

Being a landlord, however, is not as easy as it may look. First of all, it requires an understanding of the principles of operation. The specific details of the business relationship—who the tenants are, what is for rent, when the rent is due, what are the rules of the house and community, how improvements will be made—will determine how successful the relationship is. Although being a landlord may not require the same equipment as other businesses, it requires the savvy and skill of any competent business person: salesmanship, diplomacy, attention to detail, negotiation, and an understanding of finances and accounting.

Being a landlord also requires a certain psychological attitude. Unlike other businesses, this is something you can't "leave at the office," especially if you share your home with your tenant. Sometimes it seems you are "on call" during most of your waking hours and you may feel you have no privacy or time to yourself. Other times, you'll feel prompted to make a personal visit to see what's causing the loud noise/running water/banging pipes/barking/falling ceiling. Over time, you'll learn when to look the other way and when to tell your tenants to "start looking."

As a landlord, you have responsibility not only for the roof over your head but also for the roof over your tenant's. As one landlord said when he learned his hot-water heater was beyond repair, "My first thought was to call the landlord. Then I stopped and said to myself, "Wait a minute, I *am* the landlord!" Despite the bad name many landlords have, always remember you are providing housing, a basic human need. If you and the other landlords who own the twenty-four million apartment buildings in America didn't provide housing, who would? Remember, you are taking responsibility for your neighbor! For those who equate landlording with big business, it is interesting that nearly eleven million of those buildings are two- to four-family houses. It's ironic that a business in which you are providing a real service (with the additional hope, of course, of receiving a return on your investment) has a worse name than your blatantly for-profit neighborhood ice cream store!

Sometimes you'll feel defensive about being a landlord. Suddenly, you're no longer a renter—you've joined the "bad guys" and become a member of nobody's favorite profession, ready to charge actual dollars for something you own! You'll learn to swallow your biases and proudly say you're a landlord; eventually you will refrain from skirting the issue by saying you own a house with an apartment or have "some real estate." However, be prepared when people are less than fully sympathetic. Your friends won't always take your dilemmas seriously; they assume you're better off, with rents rolling in, than they are. Your tenants certainly won't take them seriously; they're not paying you to learn about the difficulties of running and maintaining a house. Gradually, you'll feel more comfortable with your role as a landlord.

Because landlording is a business, you should approach it with the same care you would exercise in any new business venture. Consider your tenants prospective business partners and scrutinize them no less carefully. This book is not intended as a substitute for the advice of your lawyer or accountant (or both). Rather, its intent is to guide the new landlord through the issues, problems and solutions to common situations. We hope it will demystify what being a landlord means—both the rewards and the responsibilities.

Our emphasis is on the three most important factors in the landlord business: the tenant, the tenant, the tenant, to borrow from the familiar real estate adage. Depending on the part of the country where you live, tenants may be easy to find; however, they are almost always hard to get rid of. You'll find, in talking to other landlords, that hassle-free landlords don't have much to say about their business but beleaguered landlords have a common complaint: their tenants. That's why the entire first half of the book is devoted to finding a tenant. You'll learn how to define what's for rent, how much to charge, how to find a tenant, how to interview and screen, and how to set up a tenancy agreement.

Equal to tenant selection in its importance is having a thorough understanding of the laws and regulations governing apartments in your community, state and country. Don't run the risk of being, as one landlord put it, "an accident waiting to happen," especially since some of the hassles landlords encounter result from their being surprised and caught unaware of various laws or dictums. Rental housing has evolved from its feudal beginnings into being a distinct consumer service, replete with warranties and minimum standards. Whether you as the landlord agree or disagree with the existing laws is not the point of this book. What is important is that individual landlords educate themselves so that they are not caught short. Experience is definitely not the best teacher! This book will tell you the general issues that commonly arise as well as where to find sources of information about local, state and federal regulations.

Every rental house offers certain financial advantages. You can expect the rent to help you meet your mortgage and tax payments. Rental income can, too, contribute toward financing needed capital improvements and repairs. In addition, rental property offers tax advantages, including deductions for apartment-related expenses and depreciation. While you're not likely to get rich by owning a house with one or several rental units, you are probably able to afford a nicer house than you would otherwise. Also, as with a single-family house, you may be able to borrow against the equity in your house to finance improvements, your vacation, your children's education, or the purchase of additional property.

The size and type of your house have more to do than you might think with determining your career as a landlord. There are advantages and disadvantages to every type of rental house. This book will focus on owner-occupied rental houses. For simplicity's sake, we have chosen to use the generic term "house" to represent the many types of houses landlords own.

What are the main types of rental houses?

The two-family house or duplex. The advantages of a two-family house are many, especially for the new landlord. First, you have only one tenant to contend with; thus, you can expect fewer demands on your time for dealing with paperwork, maintenance and general tenant business. From the outside of the house, a two-family house often looks more like a single-family house than an "income" house; as a result, you may be able to command higher rent for this homey quality than if you owned a multifamily house. Some two-family houses have separate entrances, which causes landlords to swoon with delight since separate entrances result in more privacy and quiet for both occupants.

The tax advantages are not as great as with a multifamily house. You can expect to deduct only half of your overall operating expenses. Also, you will receive rent from only one apartment.

Three-family house, triplex or brownstone. With a three-family house, you will receive two rents, which will be a real advantage when you have a vacancy since you will still have one rent coming in. Strangely enough, in a three-family house you may have more privacy than you would in a duplex; the higher the number of units, the less inclined your tenants will be to try to be chums with you. On the other hand, you may feel outnumbered or sometimes feel as if you and the tenants were interchangeable, since often the individual apartments are quite similar, one being on top of another. Three-family houses often look more like apartment houses than like traditional homes in the suburbs; but new, energetic landlords can do quite a bit to make a triplex "Home Sweet Home."

Three-family houses have been called the "milk cow" of rental housing; income is good but headaches are minimal. They are in between the two-family and the multifamily house. You can expect to deduct two thirds of your overall operating expenses in addition to being able to deduct two apartments' worth of expenses. In some locales, three-family houses are likely to be subject to rent control, which many landlords see as a disadvantage.

Multifamily house. The advantages of such houses, over and above providing shelter, are chiefly financial—herein lies the opportunity to live rent-free. However, you may be faced with having to obtain commercial rather than residential financing, even if you plan to live in the house. Also, the sheer amount of time you will have to set aside for bookkeeping, paperwork, and simple and routine maintenance is formidable. If everything goes smoothly, you will feel very close to experiencing financial nirvana, but the time-consuming business side of being a landlord will be all too apparent when something goes wrong with every unit simultaneously. For instance, if you have two vacancies, one deadbeat, and one tenant whose plumbing is backed up, you will hardly feel like a part-time landlord. In other words, a multifamily house can seem like a full-time job or business (and the income it will produce justifies your thinking of it that way).

Renting out rooms in your home. If you take in boarders, your income "unit" is your existing house and you probably do not have to alter your house to receive rental income. The amount of income is determined by the number of bedrooms. This type of rental situation is ideal for people who need extra income but have a house bigger than warranted by their present needs.

You will be entitled to similar tax advantages as with other types of rental property. You may be able to limit your rentals to seasonal rentals—for instance, only during the school year or the summer—which would enable you to have your house to yourself for part of the year.

ABOUT LANDLORDS AND TENANTS

Most tenants simply want a nice place to live; most landlords want nice responsible tenants. Granted, a few landlords do only the minimum, are inflexible, intolerant, and don't give a whit about their tenants. They give the rest of us a bad name. Some tenants fail to pay their rent, damage the apartment, or are "born-again tenants" who champion an adversarial relationship between you and them and whose discovery of pro-tenant laws has the intensity of religion. We hope this book will steer you away from them by guiding you to tenants you wish you could clone. Your tenants may prove to be the nicest people you'll ever meet. You may get to know them, become friends with them, or even marry one, who knows!

As you're reading this book, you may think we don't like or trust tenants because we urge you to proceed with caution and attention to detail. As with any other business, trust and friendship are not the issues. Rental car agencies are extremely careful before letting a customer drive off with a new car, and with good reason: they weigh the potential risk against verifiable information. You should be no less careful! You and your tenants can earn each other's trust but you both can begin by being clear in your mutual expectations.

We hope this book will guide you through the landlord-tenant relationship in addition to being a practical tool for the many issues that arise. We hope it will demystify what being a landlord means in everyday terms. A friend who was contemplating buying a rental house asked, "What's it really like—being a landlord? What do you have to keep in mind? What do you do when your tenant leaves the windows open in the rain or in the winter, or puts out the garbage on the wrong day? Do you have to think about that? How do you anticipate things? How do you keep it all straight?" We hope this book begins to answer his questions.

1

Defining the Space

You have just moved into your brownstone and are getting your-self settled and are desperate to rent out the first-floor apartment because your mortgage is due in three weeks and you've just had to replace the heating system. Without the rent, you think, fore-closure may be inevitable. So you think about where you'll ad-vertise. Perhaps you've already had several calls from people who know the apartment is vacant. Can a rent check be far behind? You think, "This'll be a snap. I'll have the tenants by Saturday and can collect the deposit money before that." DON'T DO IT.

It's important for you to take a different first step: determine exactly what is for rent and what is not. It is common for new landlords to overlook this step—they think, "I know what's for rent—the apartment downstairs." But do they?

The first step in this process is to look at the unit. How many rooms does it have? How many bedrooms? You don't have much control over the floor plan and probably can't modify it unless a dining room could be converted into a bedroom.

After you've counted the number of rooms, you should check with your city or town's housing authority—usually with the health and sanitation department—to find out what the prop-erty/occupant standards are. For instance, you may find out that a bedroom has to be a certain size and contain a closet and two windows, or that there have to be a certain number of baths per number of bedrooms. Or, you may live in a town that prohibits overnight parking—you would want to be sure and let prospective tenants know this and let them know how many, if any, parking spaces you could provide. Also, once you know the standards, you can show the apartment with confidence.

Itemize the unit itself before you even think about writing an ad. This is important for three reasons. First of all, it will help you to anticipate questions from prospective tenants and will prevent embarrassing questions during the apartment tour. For instance, when the tenant asks, "Can I put my hibachi on the porch?" you want to be ready for the question so that you can respond, "Sure," or "Sorry, the porch is unsafe/off limits," or "You can go ahead and use the porch but the fire laws prohibit you from using your hibachi on it."

Second, if you have cast a shrewd eye over the unit and have carefully observed its features, you will be in a better position to promote the apartment to a prospective tenant. Instead of walking through the apartment merely pointing out the bedrooms, kitchen and bath, you will have analyzed its selling points so that you can point out that the bath is a modern one, that the kitchen has new appliances, that the apartment faces south, that the fireplace works. What are the unit's exceptional features? You may not notice any at first, but look around. These could include polished wood floors, wall-to-wall carpeting, expansive counter space, modern appliances, built-in cabinets or bookshelves, more than one bath, good-sized rooms, charming nooks and crannies, installed draperies, more than one floor of living space, working fireplace and freshly painted walls.

Likewise, you can point out certain deficiencies in the apartment which will make you seem like an honest landlord and will possibly prevent any misunderstandings once the tenant moves in. For instance, if the refrigerator is an old one or isn't full-size, you should mention this during the tour so that the tenant doesn't move in and call you, saying "Uh, this refrigerator doesn't keep anything frozen." Or, if only three burners work on the stove, be sure and mention it.

Also, be sure to notice the condition of the unit. Do several of the rooms need painting? As you survey the apartment, decide if you are renting the unit "as is," if you are going to repaint before or after a tenant moves in, or if you will allow tenants to repaint the apartment themselves.

The third and most important reason for itemizing the unit is to determine where the tenant's space ends and where yours begins. After you have itemized the interior of the unit itself, you should then determine what the tenant's boundaries are. The apartment rental may include some areas outside of the apartment itself. These should be shown and specified during the interview. Once these amenities are used by the tenant, the tenant considers them part of the tenancy. Again, you should go through your building and assess the "public" space so that you can decide, in advance, what access, if any, tenants will have to it.

You may decide that tenants will have only the use of the interior of their apartment and will be prohibited from using any of the public spaces. As one landlord we know put it, "In addition to their apartments, my two tenants' rents include the use of the doorknob to the outside." Let's face it—chances are one of the things that attracted you to home ownership in the first place was that you wanted to have a washer and dryer, you wanted to have a driveway or a roof deck, you wanted to be able to control your space. Now that you are a homeowner, you certainly don't have to share what you've worked so hard for (though it's nice for the tenants when you do!) and certainly you shouldn't feel pressured to let your tenants use anything outside of the apartment, but you should decide in advance how you will handle it.

Don't assume that tenants will consider off limits any space outside of the immediate confines of the apartment. They won't. In fact, the reverse is true. They'll assume it's theirs to use unless you specify otherwise.

You may not want to put any restrictions on your tenants' use of public space. However, if you follow this course, you may come to regret it later. If you find that a tenant is somehow abusing the space and the privilege to use it, it will be difficult to take the space away without changing the terms of the tenancy.

Be very specific about the public space. By doing so, you will show the tenant that you have ultimate control over the space in the house, that you are aware of what the public spaces comprise, and that you have defined what the tenant is renting. If you neglect to do this, you may run into some difficulties later on. Tenants may take it upon themselves to use the yard or laundry facilities, to park in the driveway, to move their patio furniture out on the deck, or to lie down beside the pool. You may feel rigid, uptight, out of control and downright mean as you explain to a tenant that certain spaces are exclusively for your own use. However, you will feel a lot worse if you do nothing, but feel your tenant is invading "your" space. If you want your tenants to understand certain spaces are your spaces, you owe them the courtesy of telling them. Don't make the mistake of being too casual—later on you could feel territorial about every detail if you are fighting for what is rightfully yours.

If you think out beforehand how the space in your house will be used, your house will run more smoothly than if you had to keep going to your tenant and saying, "Gee, Marge, we didn't mention this, but you'll have to move your lawn furniture into the house. Yes, I know it's brand new and I should have mentioned our yard policy before you moved in and bought it, but we have to insist . . ."

What are the types of public space that you should assess before renting the unit?

COMMON HALLWAYS

Should you consider the hallway immediately outside a tenant's apartment part of the tenant's unit or is it "your" space? Unless you specify otherwise, you may find that your tenants have decorated the hallway and effectively enlarged their apartment by doing so. You probably won't object to a nice print gracing the walls of the foyer or an attractive arrangement of dried flowers displayed on a precious antique table outside a tenant's door, but what if the tenant's taste is radically different from yours? If you really would like the hallway to be decorated, why not do it yourself? Or, if you don't have the time, wait until your tenants move in and see their taste for yourself; then you could suggest, if it's appropriate, "Oh, gee, by the way, feel free to brighten up the hallway here if you'd like."

The other thing that may happen if you say nothing about the use of the hallway is that a tenant may be tempted to use the hallway to store anything from dripping wet shoes, umbrellas or cross country skis to baby carriages, brooms, mops and bicycles. These may be fine for the back hall or if the tenant lives on the top floor (and be sure to let the tenant know that) but may be less than aesthetic in a formal entry, especially if you have to walk past it every day. If you want the comon hallways kept empty, be sure and say something along the lines of "It goes without saying, but naturally, I'd appreciate it if you don't put anything in the hall here. We had a tenant once who left his muddy shoes here time after time so I just thought I'd mention it."

Before you tell a tenant that it's all right to put things in a hallway, check with the housing authority to make sure you aren't violating any fire and safety laws. Most codes prohibit placing objects or belongings in egress corridors since they obstruct safe passage.

BASEMENT OR ATTIC

Most tenants feel that their closet space is inadequate for storage. They're probably right. Most tenants will ask if they can have access to storage space in your basement or attic. This is not an unreasonable request. If you can possibly comply with it, do so—it won't cost you anything and will make your tenant happy. If you have more than one unit in your building, you will want to erect several lockable bins—one for each tenant—out of plywood and chicken wire.

You will then have to decide whether or not to allow your tenants unlimited access to this space. If so, they will be allowed to store bulky seasonal items there—bicycles, skis, scuba equipment and the like. If not, they will be able to store only large moving boxes and the like. If you allow them unlimited access, be prepared to frequently open up the basement or attic for them, which could be time-consuming and inconvenient for you.

LAUNDRY AREA

Your house may contain a laundry area in the basement, in which case you will have to decide whether or not to let your tenants use it, and, if so, whether or not you will charge them for this privilege. Most tenants would give their eyeteeth for access to a laundry area under any circumstances; providing laundry privileges makes your apartment more marketable. However, if you do allow tenants to use the laundry you might reserve certain hours or days for yourself. Few things will make you sour on a tenant quicker than a tenant who accidentally but consistently does his or her laundry just when you want to do yours. You should make the use of the laundry area part of your written agreement.

If you haven't installed laundry facilities yet, you might consider buying coin-operated appliances (available from most major appliance dealers) instead of charging the tenant a monthly fee for the use of the laundry area or including it as part of the rent.

PORCHES

Let's say your house has a spacious front porch and a first-floor rental unit. Should the tenant have the use of the porch? This is, naturally, an individual decision for you to make. If you intend to use the porch a lot yourself, it would be wise to declare it off limits unless you are eager to socialize with your tenant. However, if you know you won't use it yourself, no harm can come from allowing the tenant to use it—it's a nice perk.

Many apartments in standard two- and three-family houses have individual front and/or back porches. Unless there is a structural reason against doing so, you should include the porch as part of the unit. Be sure to point it out as a feature of the apartment even though your tenant will assume that it is in-cluded.

PATIOS

Some brownstones lack a front yard, but have charming patios or gardens in the back of the building which are entered through the apartment on the ground floor. If this is true of your build-ing, chances are you live on the ground floor so that you can take full advantage of this piece of urban greenery. If you don't live on the ground floor and if the patio is only entered through the ground-floor apartment, you'll be hard put to prohibit your tenant from using the garden area. If the garden area is entered from a common doorway, you could declare it public, shared space, in which case whoever lives on the ground floor will be able to stare at whoever is sitting in the garden!

Again, if the rental unit features a patio, be sure and mention it, along with any special instructions. Also, be sure and charge the tenant appropriately for the privilege and confirm the status of such amenities in writing.

ROOF-DECKS

Although roof-decks are not a common feature of many build-ings, they nonetheless deserve mention. If the roof is only acces-sible from the top-floor apartment it should be considered part of that apartment or off limits entirely. If, however, the roof is accessible from a common stairway, you will have to decide if all the tenants in the house may have access to it or if you want to reserve it for yourself. Whatever you decide, you would be well-advised to check with the building department to be sure that the setup on the roof complies with the city or town's codes. For instance, you may be required to install railings of a certain height (if these are lacking, they should be installed anyway!) or a special type of floor surface. Also, if you are planning to install a roof-deck, it would be wise to check with a structural engineer about whether or not the roof will support the weight.

If the rental unit does include the use of the roof, be sure and point it out as a feature of the unit.

DRIVEWAY OR PARKING SPACE

Lucky is the tenant whose apartment comes with the use of a driveway or a parking space! If you're able to offer the tenant either a private driveway or a parking space, look carefully at the size of the driveway. Will it hold more than one car? (One landlord we know would only rent to someone with a small car since the tenant's driveway would only accommodate a car of that length!) Then, after you've determined how many cars can be parked in the space, decide in advance whether to charge separately for it or to include it in the monthly rent. Charging separately shows the space is worth something, especially if you live in an urban area. (After all, you could always rent it to someone else.) You might charge per car if the space holds more than one car. Also, make it clear who will be responsible for its maintenance, and for shoveling snow in the winter. Unless you love exercise, you probably should hold the tenant responsible.

Let's say, however, your house has only one driveway or has a "piggyback" set of parking spaces. Beware! Sharing a driveway with your tenant is apt to be a hassle. That's not to say it can't be done successfully; but if you have a choice, keep the driveway for yourself, or for your guests if you don't have a car. For example, if your tenants share the driveway and park behind you, they will have to move their car whenever you want to go out. You may find yourself knocking on their door day after day to ask "Would you move the car?" Eventually, this might be too much of an inconvenience so you would discontinue the practice of allowing tenants to use the driveway.

Another way to manage sharing the driveway is to exchange keys, which minimizes the amount of contact you would have to have about the car. However, as one experienced landlord told us, "It becomes petty. The woman downstairs will get up to leave about six, so she's moving my car. Well, I know she's not going to warm the car up right. A couple of times I've been up and she's just zooming out 'cause she wants to get the hell out. Little things get at you. I'm thinking about getting a nicer car . . . However, I know if you start a car three more times a day every day of the week, it's a strain on the car. If I get a new car, I'm going to keep the driveway to myself." On the other hand, if you use your car infrequently or have to provide parking and your ideal tenant has a car, anticipate what types of problems you might have by analyzing your car habits.

Also, be sure and iron out who'll shovel before the first snow falls. Since you're both using the driveway, this can be tricky. Should the driveway be shoveled right away or by the first person who needs to get out? Should whoever shovels shovel the entire driveway or just shovel out his or her car? Your most sensible course would be to contract with a third party to shovel the drive regularly, thus eliminating possible friction over this issue. If you can't afford this course, or can't find someone to do it, you have no choice but to shoulder the responsibility yourself or share it with your tenant. You won't want to put the entire burden on the tenant! Anticipate the logistics. For instance, if your tenant regularly leaves for work an hour after you do, he may not feel pressured to shovel the driveway until he needs to get out himself. Clearly, if you are sharing the task of shoveling, you'll both have to get out and shovel so that you can get your car out.

As with the tenant's private driveway, you'll have to decide whether to charge separately for the use of the driveway or include it as part of the rent.

GARAGES

Perhaps your two-family house has a two-car garage and you decide to rent the garage along with the unit. You'll have to decide whether to charge for the garage separately or include it as part of the monthly rent. You'll also want to let the tenant know about any restrictions that may apply or about your expectations for its upkeep. For instance, is it acceptable for your tenant to use the garage for his trash, for storage, to tune up his car, to play his drums or whatever? Probably the most sensible way to present this is to say, "The garage is available to you. Please limit its use to storing your car and check with me before using it for any other purpose."

YARD

Perhaps your house has a spacious yard that you'd like to share with the tenant. Before doing so, decide in advance how you will handle its maintenance, as a yard can become a bone of contention between landlord and tenant. The ideal situation occurs when you and the tenant can each have a private part of the yard.

From a practical point of view, you have to decide who will be responsible for its maintenance. The grass will have to be cut, the leaves raked, and the garden weeded. If you share the yard with your tenants, it's only fair that you should expect them to pitch in with its upkeep. You might decide to cut the grass on a regular basis but have the tenants responsible for the leaves in the fall or for weeding. Before assigning tenants the task of cutting the grass, check with your insurance agent about your liability should they injure themselves.

If you don't use the yard but let a tenant use it, the tenant should be the one to maintain it. As a landlord who is away a lot told us, "I've got a nice yard, not fancy, but it's a good-sized yard and I fenced it in for my dog. But it turns out the dog won't go out there unless I'm there, but I won't go out in the yard because I have hayfever. I don't use the yard at all. My tenants wanted to use the yard. I said fine. They wanted a garden and it was the perfect location for a garden, it's quite open and there's a lot of sun and there's plenty of room. I'd just as soon let someone else have the use of it. However, I don't cut the grass on a regular basis because I don't use the back yard and I won't cut the grass because I spend two days in bed afterwards, [from hayfever], so when I find someone who will cut the grass for me,

I do that. But it's not a real priority for me, and, as long as I'm not using it, I don't care. If they want to use the backyard and want the grass cut, they're free to cut it or wait for me to get to getting around to getting someone to cut it. We've had to tangle with that, whether or not I should cut the lawn . . . They're not direct. They just become irritated about little things and then it comes out as to why they are irritated. We just talk about something or other and then they say, 'Well, the yard *really* needs cutting.'

"That was a pattern," he continued. "Little snipes meant to be casual but obviously not or they wouldn't bring it up . . . Next time I would have everything very carefully spelled out. For instance: 'You're welcome to use the yard but there's no guarantee that it will be cared for.' "

Another source of friction that might arise from sharing the yard is the issue of privacy. If your tenants have free access to the yard, they may decide to cook out with their guests right when you decide to sit out in the yard with *your* guests. Will this bother you? It depends, of course, on the size of the yard—in a large, sprawling yard, it will matter less than in a compact urban yard. It also depends on the personality of your tenants. Sharing the yard may lead to socializing more with them than you desire. After a hard day, you want to have a drink and relax outdoors. Next thing you know, your bubbly, exuberant tenant plunks herself down next to you. You always hope your tenant will be more sensitive than that, but may not be so lucky.

The third thing to consider is how your tenants will use the yard, or, more correctly, how you want them to use it. Tenants who are parents of small children will be anxious for the children to be able to play in the yard (chances are this attracted them to the apartment in the first place). You may be anxious for the children to store their toys inside, out of the yard and out of sight, and you should be sure to specify this and any other restrictions regarding yard use, such as not having the yard used as the playground for all of the neighborhood children

You may want to limit the tenants' use of the yard to sitting out at least until the breaking-in period is over. This will protect you from being hit in the face by your tenant's flapping laundry, or from seeing your manicured lawn trod on by your tenant's enthusiastic volleyball team!

Clearly, there are quite a number of factors you should consider before deciding to share the yard with your tenants. Once you offer it, you'll find it very difficult to take it away if the situation becomes intolerable. Most landlords we know reserve the yard for themselves. It's one of the things about becoming homeowners that they looked forward to and that distinguishes them from renters. If you do decide to share the yard, consider doing it gradually. For instance, offer the yard if you go away for a weekend or if your tenant would like to have a small barbeque sometime for a special occasion. This will make you seem very generous.

OUTSIDE THE HOUSE

Although it's unlikely you would include any other parts of your property as part of the apartment, you should be aware that some tenants will take whatever they can. Be clear about your front steps, back steps and walkways. Otherwise, you may find your tenants out on the stoop every night, having beers and socializing with their friends or sitting on a chaise longue at the foot of the stoop. In other words, they could be underfoot.

GARDEN

Perhaps you have a large yard that allows space for a vegetable garden big enough for you and your tenants. If you allow your tenants to plant in the garden but otherwise don't want them in the yard, be sure and specify this. Also, be sure and tell your tenants that you'll expect to eat like a king during the summer months!

Conversely, maybe you don't want your tenants planting their rutabagas in the garden but you expect to have a bumper crop yourself. If so, do what one landlord we know does—she lets her tenants take whatever *they* want out of the garden. With landlords like that, we're not sure how landlords got such a bad name!

RENTING ROOMS IN YOUR HOME

When you are renting out a room in your home it is even more important to define the exact space you are renting, since any wrong assumptions on either your or the tenant's part will affect you very directly and will be quite intrusive. You certainly want your boarder to feel at home but at the same time want him to realize it's your house and property.

Most landlords who rent out a room in their home offer kitchen and laundry privileges. If you don't, then you should clarify this at the time of rental and let the tenant know that you are renting only a room with bath.

If kitchen privileges are included, look carefully at the layout of the rest of the house. Does it have an open plan—does the kitchen adjoin the family room, living room and dining room? If so, decide in advance if the tenant should consider these off limits or if he would be welcome to plunk himself down in your favorite easy chair.

Also, should you restrict kitchen privileges in any way? Some landlords who aren't at their best in the mornings stipulate that the tenants can use the kitchen from 5 P.M. on but are expected to be on their own for breakfast and lunch. Others find it most workable to offer "light kitchen privileges"—the tenant is allowed to keep milk and juice, for instance, in the refrigerator and can feel free to fix himself a cup of tea or coffee or soup, but is discouraged from cooking elaborate meals. Although some landlords swear by this system, it seems to have a built-in problem: At what point does the tenant abuse the privilege? Is it all right to toast a bagel? Cook an omelette? One simple way to get around this sticky wicket is to provide the tenant with a hotplate and a small refrigerator in his or her room.

Other landlords fully expect their tenants to use the kitchen and to participate in the activities of the house, including sharing in the preparation of meals. They place fewer restrictions on the tenants' comings and goings in the house but often find it convenient to declare some space off limits.

If your house has more than one full bath, you may want to give your tenant his own bath, with the understanding that the other bath is off limits and is yours exclusively. Naturally, if yours is on another floor, it probably doesn't even have to be mentioned. If there is only one shower or tub in the house, you would be well advised to have a second one installed. Until then, you may want to set up some kind of schedule so that five people won't need to shower at the same time.

Be prepared for questions about storage and parking (see preceding sections on basements and driveways), although, in the case of boarders, chances are they may not have too much to store other than bicycles or suitcases.

FLOOR PLAN AND BUILDING LAYOUT

After you have determined exactly what is for rent, take one more look around the building. Does the layout suggest anything that might make for a smoother relationship with your tenant? Although the plan of the building probably can't be easily altered, a close look is nonetheless in order.

Entrances. Is there more than one entrance? If so, you might want to ask your tenant to use a specific one and you use another. This gives you both more privacy and eliminates unnecessary interactions. One landlord we know who has owned every conceivable type of rental property—three-family house, town house, rooming house—finally decided that he and his family would settle down and stop moving from house to house. He deliberately looked for and found a two-family house with separate entrances. His two apartments are side by side, and each one has two floors. In fact, the apartments even have separate addresses! He wasn't as concerned about his privacy as he was about the inevitable meetings in the hallway which would have required the usual pleasantries. It wasn't that he didn't like his tenant—he did. Rather, as he puts it, happily ensconced in his new house, "I did not want to get involved in a situation where my tenant felt psychologically that he had easy access to me."

Stairways. If there is more than one stairway, you might want to specify, as with entrances, that your tenant use one and you use another.

Occasionally, a building with a top-floor apartment is set up so that tenants have to walk through the body of the house—your living space, in other words—to get to their apartment. This arrangement is hardly ideal and requires careful tenant selection. If there isn't an outside stairway, you might consider having one added to the house; it will also serve as an emergency fire exit (many communities require two means of egress, anyway), or, if it is sturdy and enclosed, as the primary staircase.

Layout. Consider how the tenants' apartment, room by room, is related to your living space. Let's say you rent out the first two floors of your three-family house and live on the top floor. As you survey the layout you notice that the tenant's living room is under your bedroom. There is probably nothing you can do to alter the layout, but you can be selective about who the unit is rented to—the more tenants, the more likely your sleep will be disturbed!

Also keep in mind that "you live by the people above you." Most landlords opt to live above their tenants whenever possible. They thus don't have to live with as much noise—even if it's just the pitter-patter of an elderly woman's little feet, it's noise nonetheless. If there's anything that will make you feel like a tenant in your own house, it's listening to the tenants walk around. There are some definite pluses to living on the top floor: often it's airier and brighter and has more of a view, which is important in urban settings. More important from a psychological point of view, no one walks past your door; if you hear someone coming up you know it's someone coming to see you and you can quickly put on your landlord hat.

If your unit is below your tenant's—pay close attention to the layout. If the living room is over your bedroom and the tenants put powerful speakers on their floor, chances are the vibrations will keep you awake. One landlord we know was made miserable by his tenant's innocent habits. The tenant was a fidgety young woman whose kitchen was at the opposite end of the apartment from the bedroom and living room. She was a nervous eater and cut a constant path between the kitchen and the bedroom. All evening long, the landlord would hear her going back and forth. Finally he installed carpeting in the hallway so he could relax! Although he hated to cover up his newly polished floors, it proved to be an effective solution.

BUYING A HOUSE COMPLETE WITH TENANTS

Should you go to the trouble of defining the space for rent if you have just bought the house and the unit already has tenants living in it? Absolutely! If you know how to reach the previous owners (or if by chance you haven't actually passed papers yet), give them a call to find out what they consider the apartment's special features and whether or not the tenant had the use of any of the extras covered in this chapter. While you could take some of these privileges away since you are the new owner, it would behoove you to try to keep things the way they are as much as possible (unless you hope the tenant will move). You'll have to expect a little of "Well, the previous owner let us do this/use the yard/use the driveway/sit on the porch" from your new tenant. He or she may feel, "I was here first and it's more my turf than yours." There's not too much you can do about that kind of attitude except be aware of the extent of the tenant's former privileges and make it clear, if you have changed the tenant's space in any way, that it was one way before and now it's different.

You should evaluate the interior of the apartment in the same way you would if no tenant lived there, decide what you will do about the public spaces, and study the floor plan and layout. Since the apartment is already rented, these steps aren't necessary to "sell" the apartment or to help you anticipate questions. They are, however, essential in showing you where the tenant's space ends and yours begins. They also will be important to your evaluation of the rent the existing tenant is paying. Let's say you are going to have to charge a higher rent than the previous owner did. If you carefully define the rental space, you will be able to raise the rent in an informed way. Instead of just saying, "Well, Marge, it's a big apartment and I need a higher rent," you will instead say, "Well, Marge, it's a big apartment with a nice new kitchen and a modern bath. And don't you love having a guest room and a dining room? I've checked the rents in the area and think five hundred dollars is a bargain even with the modest increase."

After you've carefully evaluated the unit, decided what if anything is included with it, and assessed the layout of the building, you're now ready to set the rent and find a tenant.

2

How Much Should You Charge?

In deciding how much rent to charge, you should examine your fixed costs, current market conditions, local market conditions, local regulations, business expenses and anticipated operating expenses. You may be prohibited by rent control from charging more than the legal maximum, or an inherited lease may obligate you to charge a certain rent.

There are two schools of thought about how much to charge. The first is that the rent should be in proportion to the amount of your fixed costs, or PIT—principal of the mortgage, interest on the mortgage, and property taxes. (These, of course, may go up or down every year, but usually they are fixed for a year.) Thus, if you own a three-family house, your share would be one third of the fixed costs. This theory of rent setting presumes that owning a house with rental apartments enables you to own a better house than you would otherwise be able to afford—or perhaps it enables you to own a house, period. Although this theory makes it simple to calculate your tenants' rent, it does not evaluate all of the costs you must bear. Also, it may shortchange you if your PIT is relatively low.

The second method of calculating the rent takes you through all foreseeable expenses, helps you prorate them, and tells you how much the apartment will cost you. The apartment will cost more than the sum of principal, interest and taxes; costs over and above PIT have to be taken into account.

FACTORS TO CONSIDER

The rent you charge should satisfy the needs of your creditors for principal, interest and taxes. You may consider these costs to be fixed, at least for a certain term. (Incidentally, you should avoid the new adjustable rate mortgages unless they have an interest cap.) Naturally, if you bought your house "with tenants," the rent will probably have to be adjusted to meet your new carrying costs.

The rent you charge should satisfy your legal and contractual responsibilities for the tenants' health and safety. As outlined in more detail in Chapter 6, as a landlord you have specific responsibilities dictated by state and local statutes. If, for example, the state sanitary code dictates that a heated apartment must be 68° at all times, you must ensure that your equipment (the furnace) and the capital (your cash) will enable you to do this. Likewise, if you rent the apartment with a swimming pool, you must continue to provide the use of the pool.

The rent you charge should satisfy the needs of maintaining the "physical plant." The rent should proportionately cover maintenance, repair, capital improvements and basic equipment (heating system, appliances). In short, it should provide you with part of a building fund. It should be applied toward repairs needing immediate attention as well as toward long-term improvements and replacements. For example, the rent should cover the cost of replacing a bedroom radiator that springs a leak as well as a budgeted amount for replacing the wiring in fifteen years' time. You should be especially concerned with this if local statutes dictate certain improvements on a regular basis. In New York, for example, a landlord has to paint the interior of each apartment every three years; be sure your rent covers this.

Bear in mind that your house and the elements in it have a certain life expectancy and you should budget accordingly. With respect to the physical needs of the house, it is best to have a professional inspection to determine what will need to be done and when it will need to be done. Thus, if an inspection shows that a new roof will be needed in five years and will cost five thousand dollars, you should allocate a total of one thousand dollars a year from all your apartments. If you have a three-family house, then, you will prorate the charge accordingly and "charge" each apartment twenty-seven dollars per month in anticipation of this costly repair (one thousand dollars divided by twelve months divided by three apartments). It's absolutely critical to factor in this type of repair and maintenance cost if you have just bought the house, especially if it is an older house on which little recent maintenance has been done. Otherwise, you will be unpleasantly surprised on a regular basis.

The rent you charge should cover your risks as a small businessman. It should provide for vacancy, return on your investment, insurance, legal expenses, office expenses and supplies. It should also take into account the "cost of doing business"—if you have to take out a three-thousand-dollar loan to replace the plumbing, the loan will cost you in both principal and interest.

Skeptics may argue that, because many of the above-mentioned expenses are deductible as business expenses (for more about this, see Chapter 9), they don't have to be taken into account in setting the rent. Although this may be true on paper, it's still necessary for the rent to cover a proportion of your monthly cash flow because money has to be earned and spent before it can be deducted.

The rent should satisfy local regulations. If your apartment is covered by rent control, you may not charge more than the legal maximum. Although administration and enforcement of rent control regulations are often ineffective, you would be ill-advised to decide, "I'll charge just a little more—I'll never get caught." While you may not be liable for damages for any infractions, you may be hard-pressed to come up with, say, eight thousand dollars in rent surcharges and interest, as one New York City landlord recently had to after he was caught overcharging.

The rent you charge should satisfy local market conditions. Find out what apartments in the area rent for and how much demand there is for rental apartments. Check newspaper ads and local real estate agents for "comps" (comparable apartments). Remember to factor in the age and character of the house, the overall condition of the neighborhood, the type and "presence" of the house (if you own an old seaport captain's mansion, you may be able to command more rent for a small four-room apartment than you would if exactly the same amount and type of space were in a five-floor walk-up), the number of bedrooms and baths, and any amenities (driveway, fireplace, garage, yard, deck, pool, etc.) that are included. For more detail about this, see Chapter 1. If you are new to the area, you may want to go see some of the other apartments on the market to find out what your competition is. Likewise, don't hesitate to call a real estate agent for an appraisal; you may not list the apartment with the agent this time but may decide to in the future.

You have two risks in setting the rent—that you will rent the apartment at too low a rent, in which case no applicant is going to turn to you and say, "My goodness, this is so cheap!" Or, that your rent is higher than the market will bear. You'll quickly find out if this is the case, since your apartment may go unrented. In both cases, you run the risk of losing valuable income.

CALCULATING THE RENT

This step is hard work as it requires you to estimate and project, as precisely as you can, what your apartment will cost you every month. *Only when you know what the apartment will cost will you know how much you should charge.* We are going to demonstrate the principles of setting the rent by an example. Let's assume you just purchased a three-family house for $100,000. You put down 20 percent, or $20,000, and are carrying an $80,000 fixed-rate mortgage at 12 percent interest over thirty years. Your monthly payment of principal and interest is $1,050. The three apartments are of equal size, with three bedrooms, one and a half baths, and seven rooms apiece.

In order to decide how much to charge each tenant, you should itemize all of your regular and anticipated expenses and prorate the total accordingly, taking into account the "life expectancy" of the physical plant.

1. Expenses

Fixed Costs	Annual Amount	Monthly Amount	Tenant's Share (one third)
Mortgage	$12,000	$1,000	$333
Taxes	3,600	300	100
Insurance	1,200	100	33
Water & sewer	480	40	13
Public lighting	120	10	3
Trash collection	120	10	3
TOTAL:	$17,520	$2,460	$485

2. Expenses Related to Repairs and Maintenance

	Annual Amount	Monthly Amount	Tenant's Share
Roof ($5,000 every 20 years)	$250	$21	$7
Exterior painting, siding, or brick repointing ($5,000 every 5 years)	1,000	83	27
Heating system ($3,500 every 30 years)	116	10	3
Interior painting ($5,000 every 3 years)	1,666	138	46
Floors ($3,000 every 10 years)	300	25	8

	Annual Amount	Monthly Amount	Tenant's Share
Bathrooms ($6,000 every 10 years)	600	50	16
Kitchen appliances ($3,000 every 10 years)	300	25	8
Wiring ($500 every 20 years)	25	2	0.70
Site improvements ($500 a year)	500	41	13
Tools ($600 every 10 years)	60	5	1.60
TOTAL:	$4,817	$400	$130.30

3. Expenses Related to Your Business

	Annual Amount	Monthly Amount	Tenant's Share
Dues to professional organizations (two @ $100 per year)	$200	$16	$5
Magazine and journal subscriptions	100	8	3
Office in home (one room in your apartment used half of the time for business)	1,296	108	36
Telephone (used one quarter of the time for business)	72	6	2

	Annual Amount	Monthly Amount	Tenant's Share
Supplies (rental forms, postage, Xerox copies)	200	16	5
Legal consultation (16 hours @ $50 per hour)	800	66	22
Car ($200 per month; car used one tenth of time on business)	240	20	7
TOTAL:	$2,908	$242	$81

4. Capitalization

	Annual Amount	Monthly Amount	Tenant's Share
Return on investment (8.5% on $20,000)	$1,700	$141	$47
TOTAL:	$1,700	$141	$47
GRAND TOTALS	$26,945	$2,245	$748

As you can see from the preceding breakdown, the apartment will cost you $748.00, not taking a vacancy factor into account.

To calculate the vacancy factor, figure your tenant's annual rent ($748 × 12 = $8,976), add one month's rent to it ($9,724), and then divide again by 12 ($810). Essentially what you are doing is figuring a standard one-month vacancy; to get the annual rent you need you must really figure on charging for thirteen months to get twelve months' income.

VACANCY FACTOR

Tenant's annual rent	= $8,946
Additional month's rent for vacancy	+ $748
Adjusted annual rent	= $9,724
Tenant's monthly rent ($\div$ 12)	= $810

In order to cover all of your costs, you should charge your tenant a rent of $810.00. This is considerably more than what you would have charged if you had followed common wisdom and charged your tenant one third of your PIT of $1,300, or $433.00. From this ballpark figure, you can project what a tenant should earn to be able to pay your rent. One rule of thumb is that rent should equal one or two weeks' pay. If you follow this, you can figure that your tenant should earn at least $21,060 (26 weeks $\times$ $810).

After doing the above calculations, you may gasp and exclaim that the market would never allow rents that high! Clearly, you have choices. Perhaps you are a lawyer so you don't have to factor in an annual amount for "legal consultation." Or your uncle is in the paint business so you can figure interior and exterior painting at a much reduced rate. Or, you feel you can live with less than an 8 1/2 percent return on your money; after all, you counter, "I can't *live* in a money market fund." Or, you think a low rent will attract the right tenant. Or, perhaps market conditions are such that you know you would be able to rent the apartment in a flash if it became available. Only you can make those adjustments—but make them cautiously. Otherwise, you'll discover a new meaning to the word "housepoor."

Don't make the mistaken assumption that a lower-than-market rent will result in fewer demands from your tenant. We know one landlord who was looking for a very specific type of tenant and offered her a top-floor apartment at several hundred dollars less than market rate. He asserted, "If you don't charge top dollar, you won't have many demands placed on you." He was wrong—his tenant badgered him about real and imaginary faults with the apartment, many of which he had to fix—while he continued to collect his clever low rent. Some tenants may see a bargain and keep a low profile about minor repairs, but others will never let up, bargain or no bargain.

You may be able to adjust some of the anticipated costs by taking into account the tax advantages you enjoy by being a landlord (see Chapter 9).

You may also wish to make adjustments based on the apartment's peculiarities. For instance, if the first-floor apartment has a large deck and the second floor does not, you may wish to charge more for the first floor—say, $770 for the second floor and $850 for the first floor. Or, if it's a general rule of thumb in your neighborhood for tenants to pay extra for parking, you may wish to charge yours accordingly.

After you have done the above calculations, you may be pleasantly surprised to discover that the rent you should charge (i.e., what the apartment will cost) is significantly below what the market rates are. Let's assume your base rent of $810 is low; comparable apartments rent for $1,000 or more. What should you do? (If you have to ask, you probably should forget about being a landlord and engage in charity work!) Charge as close to the market rate as your conscience will allow!

Also, remember that the higher your rents, the higher your house's market value; an income-producing house is judged on the rents it can command.

THE BUILDING FUND

Before you rub your hands with glee at the prospect of collecting $1,620 per month for your two apartments when your PIT is $1,300, you should decide exactly what you will do with the $320 a month (that is, what you collect over and above your PIT). If your tenant's rent is paying you for anticipated repairs and improvements, you should treat those anticipated costs as real costs, and pay yourself the amount due for repairs and maintenance. In the case of our example, you would pay yourself at least $130.30 as a reserve against future repairs—which will surely be needed. It is of the utmost importance to maintain this building fund. First of all, the cost of many repairs and improvements is high. If you suddenly find you have to spend $3,000 on a partial new roof, you may not have the reserve and have to borrow the money, which would cost you in interest. Second, you may have to make needed repairs and improvements quickly to keep the apartment in conformity with the various applicable codes.

RENT CONTROL AND RENT STABILIZATION

If an apartment in your house is subject to rent control, you cannot raise the rent beyond the legal maximum rent, which is set by local or state law. The legal maximum rents are set, usually by a local rent board, and are computed on the basis of taxes, water and sewage disposal charges, an allowance for capital value, an allowance for operating costs, and an allowance for vacancy and other losses. Each city in which rent control is in force has a different formula for setting the rents. For example, New York has a complex formula for determining even operating expenses based on the number of apartments in the building, the number of rooms in each apartment, the age of the building and a mysterious "dollar quotient."

Although you may not be able to contest the means by which a city or town assigns maximum rents, you may have some recourse. Most rent control boards allow landlords to petition for higher rents and grant increases based on economic hardship, new services or equipment, increased cost of fuel, capital improvements and the like.

Rent stabilization establishes certain maximum rents but provides for regular moderate increases, the amount and percentage of which is determined by the rent board.

TAX INCREASES

As mentioned earlier, you may consider taxes a fixed cost since the taxes are "fixed" on an annual basis. Many leases allow you to pass any increased taxes on to your tenant by means of a "tax escalator clause" in the lease (in the case of a tenancy at will, you may pass this increase on with thirty days' notice). If you have such a clause, you may pass along any proportionate increase or decrease of the real estate taxes. Thus, if your taxes went up $600 in your three-family house, you would be able to pass along $200 per year, or $16.60 per month, to your tenants. The same procedure would apply if you received a tax abatement, except that you would be obliged to give your tenant a refund.

THE MAGIC NUMBER

If you absolutely can't see your way clear to charging your tenant what the apartment will cost you, then be sure that your rent covers at least a fair proportion of your fixed costs (principal, interest, taxes, insurance, water, sewer, electricity). But don't be afraid to try to charge what it will cost. Rents increase all the time, sometimes more than even the savviest landlord is aware of. As one landlord put it, "Every time I'd have a vacancy, I'd charge a little more. Every time I would show the apartment, I'd gulp and name the rent, half expecting applicants to say, 'You're joking!' Instead, they got the 'this is a bargain' gleam in their eye. Now, after four years of playing around with minimal rent increases, I'm finally at the point I should have been four years ago. My rents now cover the costs."

3

The Ideal Tenant

Once you've determined exactly what is for rent and how much you'll need to charge, you have to turn to the task of finding a tenant. The tenant you find or wish to find is, of course, determined in part by the layout of the apartment you are renting. If it has three bedrooms, chances are you'll want to rent to more than one person so that you can maximize the rent. On the other hand, if privacy is important to you, you may want to sacrifice something in the way of cash and let a single person rattle around in all that space! Conversely, if your unit has one bedroom, it won't accommodate a family with three children but may be perfect for a couple.

Before you actually take the next step of advertising or actively looking for a tenant, spend a little bit of time fantasizing about whom you would like to have living in your house. One landlord told us he preferred someone "rich, deaf and mute. Someone to pay twelve months in advance." Another would love to have "a Boston Brahmin who deals exclusively in art prints from India and who has an income of a hundred thousand a year." Yet another describes his ideal tenant: "a government worker who has a thick paycheck, who is sixty-five, has no children, and no pets, and sleeps all day." Most landlords have in their mind's eye an ideal tenant, and you should strive to come as close to your ideal tenant as possible when you actually rent your apartment. Bear in mind, though, that your ideal tenant probably exists only in your imagination! Even if you think you know who your ideal tenant is, take the time to read this chapter anyway. You may find yourself willing to be more flexible the next time you have a vacancy.

It's a good idea to keep your unit's layout in mind as you think about an ideal tenant. Ask yourself:

- How many bedrooms does the unit have?
- How many baths?
- How many, if any, parking places?
- Does the layout suggest a certain category of tenant? For example, do you have to walk through the second bedroom to get to the bath or is the bath off one of the bedrooms?
- Is the tenant's front door situated in such a way that you will hear it open and close? If so, you might want to decide against someone with radically different hours than yours or against a tenant with four active school-age children.
- Where is your bedroom in relation to their living room and entrance?
- Does the unit have a yard for kids?
- What floor is it on? Is there an elevator?
- Does the local or state sanitary code impose any restrictions— e.g., "X square feet per bedroom or per person"?
- Are you restricted by any local zoning laws? For instance, some communities prohibit more than two unrelated persons from living together.

Ask yourself the following questions:

- How important is price flexibility?
- Do you anticipate having to or wanting to raise the rent on a yearly basis?
- Would you be pleased if the tenant were home all day to keep an eye on the house?
- Are you allergic to any pets? To smoke?
- Do you have kids of your own whom a tenant's children could play with? Or fight with?
- How sensitive are you to noise?

Probably, by now, you've conjured up an ideal tenant who will be able to pay the rent on time and in full, will maintain the apartment and will do his or her best to keep noise to a minimum, in addition to having all of the qualities you desire. As the owner of a three-family house succinctly put it, the ideal tenant is "Someone quiet. Pays the rent on time. Assumes a sense of responsibility for the apartment, and anything to do with the house is our responsibility. But not someone who comes running every time, saying, 'I had a light bulb burn out, do you cover that?' "

The ideal tenant comes in a multitude of shapes, sizes and income levels, but there are certain general categories of tenants, each with its own advantages and disadvantages.

THE WORKING COUPLE

Many landlords consider a working couple the Cadillac of tenants. The two incomes render some landlords downright greedy! The clearest advantage of the working couple is price flexibility—if your costs increase substantially, you can raise the rent and safely assume that your tenants will not move, and that you are not causing them undue hardship (you'll soon find out if you are!).

Another important advantage is that you will have a hedge against unemployment or layoffs. If one member of the couple is out of work, you can probably still expect to collect the rent (especially if you checked their salaries before renting the apartment). Your risk is essentially cut in half.

Working couples tend to be fairly stable as tenants—they're unlikely to move out in the middle of the night. They often will stay put until they're ready to trade up and buy a home of their own. Working couples tend to be quiet, too—their entertaining may consist of quiet dinner parties as opposed to raucous bashes.

However, working couples can be more set in their ways than other tenants and may, as a result, be quite demanding. In working couples, the nesting instinct often is wed to upward mobility and can lead to many requests to improve the apartment (if it isn't already in tip-top shape) and to redecorate or change it to suit their taste. Expect to be asked: "Could we have a washing machine hookup?" "What about repapering the bathroom?" "The kitchen floor is awfully worn—would you consider some of those nice ceramic tiles?" Often the couple consider the apartment their home and are eager to make it suit their needs and tastes. Don't fault the urge, certainly, but monitor it!

If each of the two has a car, you may have to provide more parking or at least have to expect to see more cars in front of your house.

Finally, expect that no one will be home during the day and many evenings if you rent to a working couple.

THE COUPLE WITH ONE INCOME

You may wish to rent to a couple whether or not both of them are working. If only one is working, you'll lose your price flexibility but will gain by having one person home much of the time, a godsend for you if you expect to have appliances or furniture delivered.

THE RETIRED PERSON OR COUPLE

Many landlords would give their eyeteeth to rent to a retired person. As one of them remarked, "They just don't move." Moving, being as disruptive as it is, becomes less appealing as one ages. Thus, an older person is often an extremely stable tenant.

The retired tenant is also usually very reliable when the first of the month rolls around. Many retired people are on a fixed income or a pension, have few expenses (they usually aren't still paying off college loans!) and have mastered their monthly budget. You will sacrifice the ability to raise the rent freely, but the stability and reliability more than compensate for that.

In general, an older person won't be too demanding. Older persons seldom want to redecorate—they're not inclined to want to do the work themselves (nor should you let them get up on a ladder, roller in hand!) or be inconvenienced by the work being done around them. Also, they may be used to fixing things—a leaky faucet or a creaking door—so they won't bother you as much as other tenants might.

Bear in mind, too, that it is often difficult for the elderly to find decent, affordable housing because of astronomical rent increases, condominium conversions and the like—so much so that the retired tenant will no doubt be grateful and happy to have found your apartment. By the same token, you should be proud of yourself that you are providing a service to one of America's most frequently displaced groups. This positive attitude definitely gets things off on the right foot!

THE SINGLE PERSON

As with all tenants, you have to consider age and life-style when renting to a single person. A middle-aged divorced man will make for quite a different tenant than a younger "Cosmopolitan woman."

Singles as tenants bring with them a number of advantages. In general, you can expect single tenants to be quiet and to make fewer demands. This is partly because they may not be home a lot of the time and also because, for some unknown reason, they may not want to bother their landlord. This is, of course, a plus in terms of improvements but can be a definite liability if your tenant fails to notice or neglects to tell you that the roof is leaking, that the apartment is chilly, or that the toilet won't stop running.

On the negative side, singles can be quite transient. Marriage, the invitation to move in with one's lover, or a new job can lead the single person to give notice; your apartment may be a stepping-stone to greener pastures. Also, a single tenant may invite a friend or prospective mate to move in or may have frequent weekend or overnight guests; your rental agreement should be clear about roommates.

TWO OR MORE UNRELATED MEN OR WOMEN

You may want to rent your three-bedroom flat to three men or women or some mixture of these. Your main advantage will be price flexibility. You can probably command more rent from even two unrelated tenants than you could from a couple. Also, unless a single person or couple has some reason for needing that many bedrooms—let's say, an office in the home, guest room, TV room—they probably won't be interested in paying for that much space.

As with a working couple, you will have a hedge against unemployment or layoffs. If one of the roommates is out of work, chances are he or she will be able to swing the rent since the individual roommates will pay proportionately less rent than if they were renting by themselves. This might but doesn't necessarily mean that the tenant will have a lot of money in a savings account. Also, if worse comes to worse, the tenant would probably be able to borrow from the other roommates.

You may find the individual roommates are more transient than other types of tenants. One roommate gets married, so the other one decides to move back in with her folks. The roommates don't get along, so one of them decides to move out, and the one who stays then has to find another roommate.

This transiency isn't necessarily always a disadvantage. You may find the unit undergoes a lot of turnover but you never have to actually put the apartment on the market. One landlord we know rented his spacious and elegant three-bedroom apartment seven years ago to three women. None of the original tenants still live there but each time one of them moved she found someone to replace her so that the other women could keep the apartment. Even though the landlord is now on his third set of tenants, it's as if he's had a long-term tenant.

Incidentally, you should stipulate as part of the rental agreement that you will have to approve any new roommates. Otherwise, you may be in for some surprises. One landlord we know rented his large apartment to two women, only one of whom moved in. After several months the tenant decided she couldn't swing the rent and told him a new roommate was going to move in with her cat (he didn't allow pets). She also happened to mention that it was great that her new roommate was going to have the apartment fumigated before moving in because her former apartment was roach-infested. Fortunately, it was a condition of the rental that the landlord had an "approval of new roommates provision" in the tenancy; he did not approve the new tenant's rental application.

Another disadvantage of a group of unrelated tenants is that the odds are—unless you rent to three shy or friendless tenants —the group will have double or triple the number of guests over a single tenant or couple. This means you'll hear the door opening and closing more often, you'll have a higher water bill since the toilet will be flushed more often, and the kitchen sink will be used to wash more dishes. There will be more people coming and going, especially if yours is a partying group.

You may also find that your three tenants are quite demanding as individuals. Unlike a couple, who may talk over a proposed repair or improvement to the apartment before approaching you, your three tenants may each approach you about their individual requests. Three bedrooms need repainting, three radiators are not working, etc. Sometimes, however, your group of tenants may make very few demands: because they lack a spokesman, they adopt an attitude of laissez faire.

As for the upkeep, sometimes the unrelated tenants will make their bedrooms their castles and will be less inclined to care for the common spaces—living room, dining room, kitchen, and baths. This can result in more work for you when the apartment is vacated.

MEN OR WOMEN?

Should you rent to men or women? One recently divorced landlord we know said slyly, "I'd love to have a couple of women downstairs." If you have preconceived notions about women being more domestic and tidy, consider this comment from a woman who is one of the savviest landlords we know: "Surprisingly enough, my first preference is completely opposite from what I thought it would be when I first rented. Now I always try to rent to men. Which I always said I would never do. Because women are basically much messier than men, strangely enough. Men don't pick up but they don't make as much fuss, they're not around as much, they don't seem to entertain as much—as they're used to going to a woman's apartment—and they usually can fix minor problems themselves in the end. They are less transient . . . Men are the best tenants. Women get married, change jobs, fight with their roommates; guys don't have those problems. They're steady. They're not around that much to get into each other's hair so they don't need to move around and have fights with their roommates and leave. Women, generally, last a year."

Her opinion contradicts the general stereotype held by landlords: that a group of women is neater than a group of men.

A FAMILY

Especially if you have children of your own, you may think a family is your ideal tenant. Visions of your child having one or more playmates right downstairs or next door dance in your head. And with good reason: if you live in the city, it may be hard for your child to meet other children. Romantic notions aside, what *about* renting to families with children?

Families tend to be quite stable. It's enough trouble to uproot yourself, let alone moving a family with all its attendant paraphernalia—cribs, playpens, toys and bicycles. It's emotionally and physically disruptive to move, so families like to stay put. Also, a family will no doubt be reliable when paying the rent. The responsibilities of being a parent can lead to careful budgeting—except around Christmastime!

You can, however, expect increased wear and tear on your apartment when you rent to a family with children. Naturally, the age of the child is a factor—a ten-year-old is less likely to cause damage than a toddler whose toy trucks are raced on your gleaming wood floors onto your sparkling white walls. However, the same ten-year-old may be noisier than a toddler, especially on a rainy day when his parents tell him he can invite all sixteen of his friends over.

Another consideration is what a family might have to do to make the apartment child-proof. Will they want to add safety gates or cupboard locks? Will these be permanent fixtures?

FRIENDS

Should you rent to friends? Probably not, unless you don't mind becoming enemies or less friendly as a result of some land-lord-tenant dispute. On the other hand, you and your friend just might treat each other all the more carefully to prevent that from happening. As one landlord we know recounted, "Renting to my friend Sally has never been a problem. I feel bad when she comes down and says, 'I woke up at five-thirty this morning because there are squirrels in the eaves,' but I think I'd feel bad whether I knew the person or not." You may take a more active interest in your friend-tenant's satisfaction with the apartment than you would with another tenant.

Renting to a friend has some distinct advantages. You know first-hand how stable, trustworthy and clean your friend is. (It almost goes without saying that you shouldn't consider renting to a friend who is in debt, is a slob, is a troublemaker, or has been known to move out in the middle of the night!) No doubt you've even been to your friend's apartment, so you know how he or she keeps it. Also, you probably have a good idea whether or not your friend's life-style is compatible with your house poli-cies.

If your ideal tenant is someone you hope will blend into the woodwork and not bother you, then you probably will want to be extra careful about renting to a friend since your friend may want to socialize and fit into the house like a member of the family. Fortunately, this is easy enough to spell out in advance so that you both have the same expectations about how the ten-ancy will work.

However, once your friends become your tenants, it may be all too easy for them to ask you for "favors." Perhaps they'll come to you on the last day of the month and "ask" if it's all right to pay rent on the fifteenth. Or, they'll be casual about asking your permission before making improvements—"Gee, I didn't think you'd mind if I painted that wall chartreuse." Or, they'll be remiss about picking up after themselves or repairing damage— "Gee, I feel bad about spilling the paint on the floor, but what can I do about it?"

Because your friends think they know you, they might feel they can predict your reaction to certain situations, and thus take certain actions they might not take with another landlord. Plainly and simply stated: your friend-tenant might take advantage of you. Unfortunately, when this happens you are the one who ends up looking like the taskmaster. It forces you to make a difficult choice: either do nothing and say nothing because it's your friend, or be the hard taskmaster and say, "I hate that color and I never would have said you could paint that color." The situation puts the onus on you to insist that your friend clean up the spilled paint or pay the rent as agreed. It forces you to remind your friend-tenant that you are, first, the landlord, and second, a friend. When you enter into a landlord-tenant relationship, your friendship necessarily, by definition, will undergo some changes because you each take on new roles.

When you are considering friends as potential tenants, treat them as you would any other applicant. Have them fill out an application, show them the ground rules in addition to showing the apartment and chatting over a beer. It may make you anxious to ask what your friend's salary is, but not nearly as anxious as it will to discover, when the rent is three months in arrears, that your friend couldn't afford it in the first place!

THE IDEAL BOARDER

The ideal tenant who will rent a room in your home will fall into one of the previous categories, most likely a single person or a couple. He or she deserves special mention here. In contrast to some of the advantages of stability that other types of tenants have, many boarders will not be as stable—perhaps you will rent to a student or visiting professor who will be in your home for a finite amount of time. Many people who rent out rooms consider this guaranteed turnover to be a distinct advantage. It enables them to keep their distance, since all parties know that the arrangement has a time limit.

You may be an exception, but most landlords prefer to rent rooms to quiet boarders. One woman we know deliberately rented her rooms to foreign students; their lack of ability to speak English fluently prevented too much dialogue and preserved her privacy.

WHAT ABOUT STUDENTS?

We don't mean to offend anyone, but in our talks with other landlords we have found one group singled out again and again as not being ideal tenants.

College students constitute this group. Many students don't intend to settle in the city or town where they are attending college. Many students return to their home for the summer and may want to sublet their apartment. Over the summer their plans may change, so the remaining roommates will have to find a new roommate. This sense of transiency usually doesn't result in a well-kept apartment; students may not feel their apartment is a permanent home and the apartment may show it. They may not renew their lease.

Students tend to have many guests—their pals from other colleges can descend weekend after weekend, resulting in increased wear and tear, water bills, and noise.

Conversely, graduate students are often cited by landlords as being close to ideal tenants. Usually, since graduate programs are two or three years, you can be fairly certain that your tenants won't move during the course of the program. However, stay away from law students! Even landlords who are lawyers themselves follow this advice. Law students are eager to apply their newfound knowledge and are looking for a case to try out their skills. Landlords beware!

Perhaps after reading these descriptions you have changed your mind about whom you wish to rent to. Chances are, your views about who your ideal tenant is will change over time. But if you've figured out who your ideal tenant is, it's now time for you to think about how you'll find him.

4

How to Find the Ideal Tenant

Once you have decided how much rent to charge and who your ideal tenant is, you're ready to begin looking for a tenant. You should begin looking as soon as possible—either as soon as you know your present tenant is moving or as soon as you are ready to show the apartment (ideally, the apartment should be in move-in condition when you show it). Try to allow yourself at least a month to find a tenant. This will give you ample time to advertise or otherwise publicize your vacancy, set up appointments, screen prospective tenants, check references and make your decision. Although it doesn't do any harm to get the word out early that you will have an apartment available in several months' time, it's generally not advisable to advertise or list the apartment with a realtor too far in advance. Anything over two months is a bit premature, since most tenants give themselves about a month to find a new apartment. If, for example, you run an ad three months in advance, chances are you will have to keep running it for a month or two; prospective tenants who saw your ad when it first appeared will shy away from calling because they will (unfairly) assume that there must be something wrong with the apartment if it is still available! This can happen also if you post a sign on or off the property or put a sign in the window.

Tenants can come to you from five sources: referrals or word of mouth, neighborhood organizations, posted signs or notices, advertisements and rental agents. Referrals are the most personal and immediate source, while rental agents are the most far-removed. These sources are not necessarily mutually exclusive. You may use all of them at once, one at a time, or use them in some combination (for example, word of mouth plus posting signs).

REFERRALS

Referred tenants may come to you from anyone who knows the apartment is for rent: a friend or acquaintance, a neighbor, a business associate, a friend of a friend, your other tenants or other landlords. Don't forget your existing tenants—if tenants are moving out voluntarily and if you have been pleased with them, by all means let them know you would be pleased if they referred tenants to you.

Although referrals limit the number of tenants to choose from, nonetheless they are the single most-preferred way to find a tenant. The best way to get referrals is to "get the word out" that your apartment is available. Tell your grocer, your assistant, your cousin and your boss that you have a vacancy. Also, treat referrals with the respect they deserve so that the source of your referrals will continue to give you good leads.

Referrals simplify the search for a tenant—there are no ads to write, agents to deal with or signs to post. You start by calling six to ten trusted blabbermouths—a friend who works in a large company, a fellow landlord who always seems to get calls from interested tenants, your neighbor who works up the street, your photography teacher, your cousin who's a nurse at the nearby hospital, your friend the social butterfly. If you are lucky, a new tenant will be only a telephone call away. Although the process is a simple one, it isn't always the quickest way to find a tenant. It can be frustrating to sit back and wait for the phone to ring! If no one calls, you begin to wonder if all of your pals spread the word. Think about offering them an incentive—a case of wine or a nice plant would be appropriate.

Although referrals present a shortcut to the search itself, you should screen them as carefully as you would a tenant from another source—referrals aren't a shortcut to the screening process itself.

Landlords make a common mistake in renting to referrals—they confuse the referred tenant with the person doing the referring. You may think the world of Jim, your buddy from college, so much so that you overlook your prospective tenant's vague reasons for moving. Or, you might not want to rent to Jim's former girl friend because she's out of work, but you succumb to the temptation to think, "Well, Jim wouldn't have sent her our way unless she was a good risk." *Don't be too sure!* Jim may have only casually mentioned to her that he knew of an apartment for rent. Jim may also, of course, have given her a sales pitch on your apartment. Treat Jim as you would any other reference—check with him about the prospective tenant. Remember: you aren't renting to the person doing the referring. Tenants must be evaluated on the basis of their qualifications.

Find out how well your prospective tenant knows your source. Are they best friends? Long-time business associates? Or did they meet just last weekend at a church supper? If they barely know each other, it's even more incumbent on you to screen as though the referral answered an ad or came to you from some other nonpersonal connection. One new landlord we know was tickled when he rented to a couple referred to him by trusted friends. The tenants turned out to be less than ideal—their rent check bounced several times and their dog chewed on the front door of the apartment. When he mentioned to his friends that the tenants weren't working out as well as he hoped, he discovered that his friends knew the tenants through a mutual friend and had only just been introduced when they were told about the apartment.

It's worth mentioning here that even though your sources' credibility is at stake, if they steer a bum tenant your way they probably won't back you up if a problem arises. This is just as well—the last thing you need is a friend getting in between you and your tenant. On the other hand, you may feel irritated that Jim sent you some deadbeats.

Consider how well you know the source of the referral. Do you have a personal relationship, or are you connected via some large organization such as the PTA? Ask yourself if you would rent to the referrer. If not, then you definitely should look elsewhere for another tenant. How much trust do you have in your source's judgment of people? How have other referrals from that source worked out for you?

You also should consider the issue of privacy. Let's say the neighborhood busybody—a woman who has been *dying* to see the inside of your house and to know how much rent you charge —refers a tenant to you. If you show the apartment to the referral, your neighbor will get what she wants. Since your tenant will be able to observe you at close hand and may discuss your doings with your nosy neighbor, this is something to think about. Likewise, your good friend Jim might refer one of his other friends to you. The personal connection may serve to keep you and your tenant honest, since you both value Jim's friendship and don't want him annoyed if the tenancy goes sour. On the other hand, it may be a little awkward if you both see Jim socially; you each might feel obligated to include the other, thus blurring the lines between landlord and tenant. You each might feel you have less privacy than if you rented to a total stranger. This isn't just a paranoid feeling—chances are each of you will tell Jim more about the other than if you were strangers. For instance, your tenant may tell Jim all about your vacation plans or even that you have a new boyfriend. Your tenant isn't being malicious, merely conversational, but it may annoy you nonetheless. Conversely, you may come to feel that you are all one big, happy family. When you do feel this way about a tenant who comes to you via a referral, count yourself as blessed.

NEIGHBORHOOD ORGANIZATIONS

A second source of tenants are neighborhood or community organizations, including but not limited to church and civic associations, the PTA, parents' groups, sports institutions, your health club, college organizations and the like. Most neighborhoods have one or more galvanizing institutions, whether it be a church discussion group, a garden club or a political campaign center. In addition to strengthening the community, your involvement in one of the aforementioned organizations can lead to good tenants. It will lead to the word-of-mouth referral, which is the preferred means of tenant selection. Also, organizations often have a monthly newsletter or agenda that can be used to advertise your apartment. Finding a tenant through neighborhood organizations limits you to tenants who are connected to those organizations but also gives you some direct connection with prospective tenants—less direct connection than referrals but certainly more immediate than placing an ad in the city's newspaper.

Let's say you're new to the community. How do you find out about local organizations? Local newspapers, as opposed to city-wide papers, often tell of community meetings. If you live in a college town, you would do well to seek out the college newspapers.

Try to determine if your neighborhood has an activity center. Because there is an apartment shortage in many communities, community organizations have taken it upon themselves to find housing for their members. If the neighborhood revolves around the church, see if it has a system of apartment referrals. If the neighborhood has a lot of children, chances are a school is the hub of adult activity. Go to the playground and inquire. If there is a local drama club, find it.

Don't be afraid to join the local tenants' organization, either. Often the tenants who are dissatisfied are those who join, so you may want to be wary of anyone who's too much of a complainer. However, tenants use the meetings as a network for finding apartments, too; they might be pleased to hear you have one for rent, and may perceive you as a landlord interested in tenants' issues. You can thereby establish yourself as a landlord interested in tenants.

There is a bonus for landlords who seek out a local organization as a source of tenants. They're often able to find an organization whose needs and interests dovetail with their own. Thus, in addition to finding a tenant, the landlord becomes involved in something new, learns or improves a skill, and meets people with similar interests.

POSTED SIGNS OR NOTICES

Posting a sign about an available apartment is a more public method of finding a tenant than relying on word of mouth or neighborhood organizations. Where the sign is placed will determine the pool of tenants you will be able to draw from. Clearly, prospective tenants have to see the sign to find out the apartment is available. You can thus post a sign in a public place but still be limited to a relatively small group of people.

Signs have their advantages and disadvantages as a source of tenants. On the plus side, you're limited to someone who has seen the sign; a strategically placed sign designed to attract your ideal tenant may indeed result in a good tenant. A sign is an excellent way to find a tenant if you live near a hospital complex or a university. Signs are usually free—the exception might be a sign on the bulletin board of a college housing office (although, since you are providing its students a service, you might challenge the charging of a fee). If you post a sign at your local college's housing department, you can specify what "type" of tenant you want—graduate student, undergraduate student, instructor, professor—because colleges are not commercial establishments. Also, the response time often is quick. One landlord who regularly goes through Harvard's Housing Office finds his tenants within a day of putting up his signs. As he says, "Colleges attract people from other than the immediate locale. Those people need to find a place to live without necessarily being in the area for three months to find it. So they put their name in the housing office, and in [one] of my cases, one couple came, they both actually came from California and wrote to the housing office saying what they wanted and came here with three or four apartments to look at. It was all set up by the housing department."

Since you aren't paying for the sign itself or for the number of words (as you would in a newspaper ad), you can be as descriptive as you want. If you run a newspaper ad, you are likely to be succinct and limit yourself to the facts about the apartment (rooms, rent, etc.), whereas if you put up a postcard on a bulletin board you will be able to list the positive features of the apartment. For instance:

APARTMENT AVAILABLE

Central Avenue location. Charming, sunny, two-bedroom apartment in duplex owner-occupied 1800 house.
Living room with fireplace, dining room, eat-in kitchen, two baths.
Newly painted throughout, polished hardwood floors.
Separate entrance, rose-trellised porch. Parking.
Fenced yard. Dog or cat OK.
$400 plus heat. See for yourself!
Perfect for working couple.
Security deposit and references required.
Available August 1.

versus a typical newspaper ad:

2-bedroom apartment. Parking.
$400 plus heat. Pets OK.

The smaller ad shows what you might put in the newspaper. By being very descriptive in your notice, you will also save yourself from calls by curious prospective tenants who want to know the details of the apartment—e.g., "Where is it?" "Does it come with—?" "What is the condition of the apartment?" "What floor is the unit on?"

On the negative side, signs limit your pool of potential tenants. If you are in a hurry to rent the apartment, you may want to expand the audience who reads the ad. Second, you have no direct control over your sign, which someone may take down or cover up. Thus, be sure and check it periodically. Third, and most important, most tenants who are looking for an apartment will look in more conventional places, such as a newspaper or the office of a rental agent. This isn't always the case—perhaps your local supermarket or the college housing office is known for its bulletin board, in which case tenants will be drawn to it.

Signs can be posted on the bulletin board of your local market or church, at your health club, on the employee bulletin boards of hospitals or places of business (including your own), and at local schools, colleges, libraries and restaurants. If you are posting a notice at your place of work, you may want to be discreet about the rent you will charge. If you live in a college town, you may, at first, be overwhelmed by the number of bulletin boards —head for the housing office, any student's first stop for apartment hunting.

Be sure your sign is neat and legible. The heading should be legible from five feet away—you want to attract people to come over to the bulletin board and read it. If the exterior of your house or your street is particularly charming, photocopy a photograph of it directly onto your sign. Include your telephone number along the bottom, "fringe" style, so that the prospective tenants can tear off your number. Do whatever you can to make it as easy as possible for your tenant to find you!

A SIGN ON THE PREMISES

Unless you live on a very well-traveled street, you shouldn't rely on a sign on your property to bring tenants your way. Not only will finding a tenant by this route be a long process; it may be a hazardous one, because anyone driving or walking by might think the apartment is vacant and therefore an easily accessible burglary target.

Let's say, however, that posting a sign on the property is a popular and preferred way to find a tenant in your locale. You have a choice of putting a sign in the window (provided it's on the first floor) or putting a sign on or in front of the house. You can afford to be simple and to the point in the wording of your sign:

> Apartment for rent
> Inquire within (ring apt. 2)
> or call 999-0999

If you have more than two apartments in your house, be sure to specify what doorbell to ring. Otherwise, your other tenants will be unnecessarily bothered and you may miss a potential applicant.

So that your sign has the greatest possible impact, consider posting the sign on just one weekend. Team the sign up with several signs on the nearest main street which say:

> Apartment available.
> See it TODAY and tomorrow at 186 Pacific Street.
> Take next left.

Limiting your sign time to two days will give you a very quick idea if this method is effective. If it isn't, simply take down all the signs and use one of the other sources for prospective tenants.

ADVERTISEMENTS

The fourth source of tenants is the newspaper advertisement. It is the most public source and has many advantages. First of all, the ad will reach a large number of people on the day it runs. Second, you as the landlord will know within several days how effective the ad is in luring prospective tenants—often on the day the ad runs you will be deluged with calls (assuming you have a desirable unit to rent!). Unlike the other sources of tenants previously discussed, which often entail more time-consuming processes, a newspaper ad will not try your patience, make you wonder when the phone is going to ring, or if your buddy Jim ever told his friends that your apartment is available. This speedy response time from advertisements is invaluable when you are in a hurry—and what landlord isn't?—to fill a vacancy.

You know very quickly whether your ad will result in a tenant or not.

The primary disadvantage of advertisements is their cost. You can expect to pay from five to ten dollars for an ad in a neighborhood newspaper and up to seventy-five dollars for an ad (depending on size of ad, number of days, etc.) in a major city newspaper. However, don't forget that the cost of the ad is a business expense and is therefore deductible.

Also, and this isn't exactly a disadvantage, you may be overwhelmed with applicants, which means you'll have to be an efficient screener.

An advertisement lacks the personal connection that makes referrals and neighborhood organizations appealing sources of tenants. However, your choice of a newspaper may compensate for this lack. If you run an ad in a local, neighborhood or regional newspaper, you will clearly limit your pool of prospective tenants to its readers. People who live in the area are likely to respond.

Ads in local newspapers—even if they are weeklies—are likely to cost less than citywide papers and are just as likely to produce results. It's a good idea to start with them when you go to advertise. Also, check to see what the paper's biggest circulation day is. Many metropolitan papers have a huge Sunday readership, but smaller papers might have a large circulation on, say, their "Food" day. Also, check to see if the paper offers special rates. For instance, you might pay only a little bit more for an ad that will run on Friday, Saturday and Sunday than if you ran it on Sunday only. You also might want to run an ad in a special interest newspaper—aimed, say, at readers of certain political persuasions. However, these papers are often of limited circulation and may not be as reliable.

Naturally, if you are advertising only one apartment, newspaper advertising is probably as "big" as you would want to go. However, keep an open mind. One savvy landlord regularly charters a plane that flies over the university football stadium during games. Thousands of viewers see the message: Brownstone Realty Rents Property. So don't limit yourself unnecessarily to print media!

How detailed should your ad be? You might be tempted to keep your ad short and to the point to keep your costs down. However, a descriptive ad will screen tenants for you and will attract prospective tenants who have decided to call because the description appealed to them.

Before you write your own ad, look through the local newspaper to get some ideas. Figure out what draws you to certain ads and incorporate some of their descriptions in your ad. While you're at it, check the apartments wanted (or, in the case of a room in your home, situations wanted) section of the paper to see if there are any promising prospects. If so, you've just saved yourself the cost of an ad. Although it's unusual for people to advertise that they want an apartment, it occurs most often with transferred businesspeople or professors who need a place to live in a hurry.

At the very least, your ad should include the location (town and neighborhood—e.g., "Beacon Hill" or "Park Slope"), number of bedrooms (this will let the tenant know how many occupants can comfortably live there), the monthly rent, and when the apartment is available.

The following elements are also commonly included:

- the type of building—e.g., two-family, brownstone
- total number of rooms or the names of the rooms—e.g., "2-bedroom apt., lr (living room), dr (dining room), kit. (kitchen)," or "6-rm apt., 2 br (bedrooms)"
- the specifics of the kitchen—"modern kitchen" or "dw" (dishwasher) or "d & d" (dishwasher and disposal), "eat-in kitchen," "new appliances," "gourmet kitchen"
- the condition and number of baths—"modern," "CT" (ceramic tile)
- thumbnail adjectives: sunny, charming, spacious, elegant, huge, small, cozy, deluxe, clean, roomy, quiet, remodeled or renovated
- whether the house is owner-occupied
- what the special features are:
  fireplace(s)
  porch or deck
  nice view

for a tenant's eligibility based on income, credit references and the like. You have no obligation to rent to a veteran, for example, simply because he is a veteran if he doesn't meet your other objective criteria. In other words, you can exercise your own freedom of choice while staying within the law.

Bear in mind that you can get into trouble if you do not treat all tenants equally. It's one thing if a tenant volunteers information about any of the criteria that are prohibited by law. For example, if a prospective tenant calls and says "I'm interested in your apartment because it's in the Italian section and I'm Italian and love the little markets," that's certainly fine. You as the landlord, however, can't say, "Oh, I see your name is Roma. Is that an Italian name?" This kind of question isn't allowed because it isn't directed at all tenants. Likewise, if a tenant says, "I would like to see the apartment but I can't come over until after church on Sunday," you can't ask, "Oh, what church?" This kind of caution frustrates many landlords because it inhibits free conversation but it's to your advantage to be aware of the laws in case a refused applicant ever charges you with discrimination. Also, because of media attention and the civil rights movement, you are aware of racial discrimination; you may be unaware of the strictures against discriminating on the basis of religion or sex or national origin.

A case against you for discrimination would be expensive to defend. If you were found guilty, you might have to pay damages to the refused tenant for mental anguish and you might have to pay moving charges as well. This is all the more reason to make your decisions based on objective criteria secured through a written application. This way you can be sure you get exactly the same information from everyone.

Before actively advertising or interviewing for tenants, you should find out if your state and city have any additional discrimination statutes so you can be sure to comply. You should also find out if the state/city statutes apply to all buildings or if there are any exceptions—e.g., an owner-occupied two-family house or a brownstone with less than three rental units. Fortunately, most newspapers prohibit discriminating advertising; the staff of the classified ad desk can be very helpful when you are preparing an ad.

State and city governments are set up differently nationwide, which means you may have to make several calls before you reach the right department to find out what the laws are. For starters, call and state your business right at the beginning: "I'm a new landlord and want to find out what the state or city laws are about rental housing and discrimination. Could you please direct my call?" The following offices may give you the information you require:

- the state's attorney general's office (sometimes the consumer protection division can answer)
- the state's commission against discrimination
- the city housing court
- the city housing authority
- professional landlord or real estate associations

For more information about the federal statutes, contact the Fair Housing and Equal Opportunity Division of the U.S. government's Housing and Urban Development Department. Each of the offices has a Compliance Division that can answer specific questions about the law.

5

Screening and Interviewing

You are about to entrust part of your valuable real estate to an unknown person, a tenant. You should do all you can to find out as much as you can about prospective tenants before offering them the apartment. You should be extremely careful in the process of evaluating what you find out. You should be at least as scrupulous as an employer is before hiring a new employee or as a rental car agency is before letting a stranger drive away in a new car. The tenant you choose is the most important ingredient in how the tenancy will go. Incidentally, if you just bought the house and have existing tenants, plan to follow the guidelines set out in this chapter.

Once you've finally opened the floodgates (you hope) and begin to respond to the many inquiries about your apartment, you may be impressed with the first person who inquires. Landlords are often caught in a rush to get income to meet monthly mortgage payments and make the mistake of renting to the first person who seems appropriate. Even if you eventually end up by renting to that first applicant, you should follow Rule One of the screening process:

Rule One: Always have a choice.

Remember: you have what the tenant wants! Landlords break this rule for many reasons: they're afraid their ideal tenant will find another apartment; a week has passed, their ad has only generated one call, and they're afraid they'll lose rental income; the mortgage is due tomorrow; the applicant came through a referral and the landlord is afraid the referrer will be insulted if anyone else is interviewed; or, the landlord didn't think finding a tenant would be as easy as only interviewing one person. Don't fall into any of these traps—you'll feel better about renting to your tenant if *you* choose that tenant over someone else. Likewise, if your tenants know they have won the apartment over some other applicants, they'll have warm cozy feelings about you right from the start.

PHONE SCREENING

Your first contact with your future tenant will most likely be by phone. Your job in this initial telephone conversation is to eliminate right away any tenants who for one reason or another are unsuitable and to determine if you and the applicant have anything further to discuss.

The first thing to establish is how the tenant heard of the apartment. If you find out the source—whether it was a friend or an advertisement—you will have some idea of what the applicant knows about the apartment. For example, if applicants say, "I saw the ad in the *Phoenix,*" you will know instantly how much information they have about the apartment. On the other hand, if an applicant says, "My friend Joe told me you have an apartment for rent," you will have no idea what Joe said about the unit. Also, you will be able to determine how effective your various ways of finding a tenant are—did the free bulletin board at the hospital result in more inquiries than your paid advertisement? Having this information will make your job that much easier and more efficient the next time you have a vacancy.

The second step is to describe the apartment in detail and to let the tenant know what the financial requirements (monthly rent and deposit money required) of the tenancy will be. Tell prospective tenants the precise location and its proximity to public transportation. Then, tell them about each room, giving them an idea of the rooms' sizes and special features. Be sure and give the total number of rooms, what floor the unit is on, and any other pertinent information (see Chapter 1). Be candid, too, about its drawbacks—whether it's noisy, has small rooms, or is dark. Even if the prospective tenant saw a descriptive ad, you should repeat what was in the ad and elaborate on it. Chances are most applicants are making a number of inquiries in order to find an apartment and have forgotten what your ad says by the time they have finished dialing your number! Also, in the case of a referral by someone you know, don't assume that the referrer has fully described the unit to the applicant.

Giving a detailed description on the telephone has a twofold purpose. First of all, you will be able to eliminate any tenants whose needs are not met by the description. Secondly, you "sell" the apartment, so that by the time you show it your tenant's appetite to see it will have been whetted.

After running through what the apartment is like, you'll want to state what the rent is and what is included (utilities, heat, etc.) and to specify how much money will be required in advance—first month's rent, last month's rent and security deposit, for example.

Then, find out what the prospective tenant's needs are: when he needs the apartment, how many bedrooms he requires and for how many people, if he has pets, if he needs parking, and if what he can afford is less than what your apartment rents for. You may discover that what you have to offer and what he needs are worlds apart and, if that is the case, you can end the conversation right there. Otherwise, get to the most important question of the telephone screening—find out the applicant's economic situation by finding out his or her gross monthly income. As a general guideline, it should be four times the rent—if it is only two or three times as much, you will probably want to eliminate him as a candidate. Ask if the advance money would pose any problems for him. However, decide in advance that you won't waive this requirement for anyone and stick to it. Finally, find out why the caller is moving—has the building been sold, is his apartment too small, is she getting married or expecting a baby, are they being evicted (they probably won't tell you!).

After you and the applicant have exchanged the necessary information, you both will have to decide if a personal interview and tour of the apartment is the next step. If you know your apartment won't satisfy the applicant's needs, don't be afraid to say so and thereby save yourself valuable time. You could conclude the conversation by saying, "Well, from what you've said, it doesn't sound as if my apartment is the right one for you because it is too small/too expensive/doesn't have enough parking."

Plan to schedule all interviews around the same time so that you will be able to make your decision promptly and not keep anyone waiting too long unnecessarily. Also, let any applicants know you plan to show the apartment to other people; this gives you an "out" if you decide against them and gives you breathing room to make your decision.

THE INTERVIEW AND APARTMENT TOUR

The personal interview, in conjunction with a written application, should be the source of *all* important information about prospective tenants. It can be conducted during or after the tour of the apartment and should always take place in the apartment, as opposed to your own unit. The purpose of the interview is to gather and dispense information, both quantitative and qualitative, that will enable you to decide on a tenant. The interview is the beginning of the landlord-tenant relationship. Thus, it sets the tone for that relationship.

To protect yourself from charges of discrimination and to help you remember who said what, you'll want to get the same information from all applicants. The simplest way to do this is to have all applicants fill out a written application, which will help you keep track of what was said and will serve as a permanent record for your files. Separate applications should be filled out by each adult who would live in the apartment (remember: antidiscrimination laws prohibit you from asking marital status, so even if only one spouse is working you'd be well advised to get two applications). The application should ask for name, present address, present employment, other sources of income, terms of present lease or rental agreement (amount of rent, heated vs. unheated), the names of all persons who intend to occupy the apartment, and if the applicant has any pets. It should solicit information about bank accounts, credit references and sources of other income. The application will give you at-a-glance information about a prospective tenant. A sample application can be found on page 83.

Pay close attention to the applicant's sources of income. One shrewd landlord we know recommends, "I'm particularly conscious of what income is attachable and what income isn't. For example, welfare income isn't attachable, and Social Security's not attachable. You can get somebody who says, 'Well, I make five hundred dollars a month' when they get three hundred in Social Security, so if they leave you're not going to be able to collect on two hundred dollars." Remember, if your tenants skip out on you and you sue them in civil court for any back rent they owe, they can be found guilty and their income or bank account (or even their car) can be attached to pay their debts.

You want to set a good example as well as looking the part of a landlord. Dress neatly but conservatively. Leave your designer suit on the rack—after all, you don't want to look too prosperous! Be firm but friendly. Be confident—after all, you have something—your apartment—that the tenant wants.

As you interview the tenant and show the apartment, put on your salesman's hat. Don't be apologetic about any of its features. Instead, be positive about its features and about each of the rooms. Avoid saying, "Here's the bathroom. It'll do. Sorry it's not modern." Turn the situation around by saying, "Aren't these old claw-footed tubs charming!" Don't say, "I know this wallpaper's atrocious but here you are." Rather: "The last person who lived here got a blue rug which made the wallpaper look fabulous" or "This wallpaper is quite serviceable and in good condition, as you can see, but I would be willing to let you paint over it."

In addition, be direct about your house policies as you walk through. If the yard is off limits, don't say, "Oh, by the way, we've had to decide that you can't use the yard because we are nuts about our privacy," but rather, "The use of the yard is not included as part of the apartment. It is reserved for our use." In general, don't feel compelled to offer explanations for your policies unless asked. Even then, don't allow yourself to be put on the defensive—and be wary of the applicant who tries to make you feel guilty! Reject that applicant immediately because that kind of attitude of mistrust will only cause you serious problems and misunderstandings later on.

In addition to finding out verifiable and quantitative information about the prospective tenant, you will also want to assess the tenant qualitatively. You might want to ask:

- What is your relationship to the person who referred you to the apartment?
- Why are you moving?
- How long do you intend to stay in the area? In this apartment? (You want to know if this is a long-term or short-term tenant.)
- What do you like and dislike about your present apartment? Describe it.
- What were some of the house policies?
- What is your taste in music? Do you play any instruments yourself?
- What is your present landlord like?
- Do you entertain a lot?
- How does your landlord collect the rent?
- What do you like about this apartment?
- Is there anything you don't like about it?
- Do you anticipate having any long-term guests? (Remind the tenant that you would rent only to applicants.)
- Do you expect to have many weekend guests? Any long-term guests?

- Do you go away a lot? Do you intend to be away from the apartment for a long period of time (over two weeks) in the next six months?

From the applicants' responses to these questions, you'll be able to form an opinion about them and to judge whether their life-style is compatible with yours. When they answer, do they look you in the eye? Do they falter when answering any of the questions?

Naturally, you don't want to act like a drill sergeant during the interview. Instead, use "the best of pop psychology in thirty seconds or less." Get the prospective tenant to talk about his or her lifestyle and habits. One landlord we know recommends: "Get on a very social basis with the applicants immediately and get them relaxed. Start, not necessarily asking questions, but get them talking. I found out in just getting them talking you get a lot of information. They're relaxed and think they have the power-hold. Sit down and put in a good hour or half an hour or forty minutes with them and it's as though they think they have the apartment and just talk while you find out a lot."

You should give the applicants a copy of your rental agree-ment and house policies for them to peruse while you are show-ing the apartment. Many landlords wait until a tenant has moved in before going over the house policies. Naturally, once the tenant moves in, you may want to go over the rules more carefully, but you want to find out during the interview if the tenant resists any rules or won't be able to abide by one of the rules of the house (see Chapter 7). Showing the tenant the list of rules during this initial interview saves you from the tenant who asks, "Why didn't you mention that I would have to light the coal furnace every morning?"

Pay attention to the clues tenants give you about themselves as you show them the apartment. They are a critical gauge for your future relationship. Their initial reactions to the unit and to the house rules will be a good indication of their future attitudes as tenants. For instance, if your agreement specifies that the tenant shovel the driveway, you may be in for trouble later on if the applicant turns to you and says, "You mean Cindy and I will have to shovel that *long* driveway ourselves? Shouldn't that be

your responsibility?" Does the applicant make this kind of re-
mark about other house policies? Ask the tenant if he or she
would have trouble following the house rules. Listen closely:
does your prospective tenant quibble with, complain about or
pick apart your written policies? If so, this may be the sign of a
dormant uncooperative or belligerent attitude.

When you begin the apartment tour, preface it by telling the
applicant that you are renting the apartment "as is," unless you
plan to let the tenant make improvements or plan to have them
made yourself. You should always, repeat always, tell the tenant:

> You will be renting what you see here. Look around.
> You are not renting some fantasy or dream apartment
> but exactly what you see here, as you see it today.

It's critical to state it baldly—that way you preclude the tenant
from misunderstanding what you meant. One landlord we know
even goes so far as to say, "This is the apartment you will rent. I
want you to look at the walls and the ceiling, the mantles and
the doors and the floors and everything. This is the way the
apartment is right now and we're not contracting to redo anything."

Tenants sometimes get so carried away with the beautiful view
or with the way the existing tenant has decorated the apartment
that they have a real shock when they move in with their few
pieces of furniture. Somehow they imagined it would look different. Their immediate response is to want to do *something* to
transform the apartment into a place that meets their expectations. They pick up the phone and make request after request.
There's no guarantee, of course, that making the key statement
will keep all such tenants away, but it will certainly enable you
to give the proper response later: "As you'll recall, Mrs. Smith, I
told you that what you see is what you get."

As you show the apartment and go over the aspects of the
rental agreement, pay attention to the questions the applicant
asks. Are they picky or reasonable? Questions like "Does the
refrigerator come with the apartment?" or "How much is the
gas per month?" or "Is this a southern exposure?" or "Is there
any place to store my bicycle?" are all reasonable and show the

tenant is paying attention. On the other hand, "Will two trash containers be sufficient?" is picky.

At some point during the interview, the prospective tenant may make some requests. Again, determine if they are reasonable or picky. The applicant who is confronted with a room with badly peeling wallpaper can be expected to ask, "Will this room be painted before someone moves in? May I paint it myself?" However, the tenant who walks through the apartment casting a decorator's eye should be scrutinized. Be wary of the applicant who turns to you and says, "I just hate wall-to-wall carpet. Could I tear it up and redo the wood floors underneath? Wood will show off my Chinese rugs so much better." Or, "These white walls aren't my taste at all. What would you think about painting the living room something exotic?" Or, "My other apartment has a dishwasher. Would you install one here—I just can't live without one."

In general, think carefully about renting to prospective tenants who make more than two substantive requests, since there's an excellent chance such tenants will have many other such requests once they move in and will never be satisfied with the four walls around them. If they are demanding during the initial interview when they should be putting their best foot forward, think about how demanding they will be once they have their foot in the door and have settled in!

As you walk through the apartment, pay attention to the applicants' reactions. Are they generally enthusiastic and appreciative? Do they exclaim, "What a lovely room!" "Wouldn't our couch look terrific here!" "What good condition everything is in!" "A modern bath at last!"? If so, that's a good sign. Conversely, are they overly critical and negative, perhaps turning to their roommate and asking, "What's that funny smell?" or saying, "I've never seen such an atrocious color for a carpet!" or "Not much counter space in the kitchen, plus these cabinets are so tacky!"? Anyone who would show such insensitivity to you as the owner doesn't deserve to live in your building. On the other hand, as we'll discuss in Chapter 7, it is important to have your rentals in tip-top shape so that you don't have to hear that kind of criticism! However, be sure and point out negative features during the tour as well; bring up temperamental air condition-ers, noisy neighbors, the lack of laundry facilities and the like.

Finally, what is your prospective tenants' general appearance? Are they well groomed and clean—not necessarily fashion plates but looking as if they care about themselves? You should evalu-ate how they appear, just as an employer would use personal appearance as one of the criteria in hiring someone. Ask yourself if the applicant looks like someone you want to have living in your house. Looks shouldn't, of course, be the only factor you consider—you'll have the other objective criteria on the applica-tion form and your sense of the kind of person this is from the applicant's questions and criticisms—but they are one more gauge of a person's suitability. We once answered the door and found an applicant wearing a short-sleeved, cut-off sweatshirt and carrying a beer in his hand. Needless to say, we didn't rent to him.

It's a pity you can't require an inspection of the tenant's pres-ent living quarters to see up-close how he or she lives. You can, however, try to arrange an invitation. Once we were on the fence about whether to rent to a prospective tenant who had a cat. We told her we were concerned about the cat scratching the newly polished wood floors and were promptly invited to visit her in her apartment so that we could see for ourselves that the floors there were in good condition. We took her up on it, rented the apartment to her, and never regretted letting her have her cat. You probably won't get this kind of invitation from a confirmed slob, so if you get it you're probably assured your applicant has nothing to hide. At the very least, take the time to drive by the tenant's apartment—it will show you the environment the tenant has been living in.

At the end of the apartment tour, offer prospective tenants the opportunity to fill out an application (there is no sense having them fill it out until they have seen the apartment). We find it's helpful to have clipboards and pens available, too. Some land-lords take deposits at this point; others wait until they have made their decision.

ROOMERS AND BOARDERS

When you are renting out a room in your home, you'll want to evaluate the tenant's financial status carefully, as you would with any tenant. However, you'll also want to pay special attention to compatibility, particularly if you include kitchen or other house privileges as part of the rent. If the applicant has an accent you just can't stand, has an unusual twitch, or has a different standard of personal cleanliness than you do, no number of financial assets or job stability is going to let you ignore these idiosyncracies. Just as many a marriage has ended over the proverbial tube of toothpaste, many a boarder situation has ended because of incompatibility.

Specifically, you'll want to question the applicant about his or her personal habits, including asking some downright nosy questions about boy/girl friends, drug use, smoking, and other personal habits such as weird diets or routines. Also, if you rent out more than one room in your home, be sure and evaluate how this applicant would get along with the people you already have "on board." If yours is a communal house in which all the boarders participate in cooking and cleanup, be sure and mention this during your initial conversation. Find out what the applicants' special needs are to make sure they would fit in.

NARROWING THE FIELD

You've seen a handful of applicants and don't have any more interviews scheduled. You're now ready to take the plunge and make the decision to let someone rent your apartment. If you've screened people carefully by phone, paid close attention to the details of the interview, and requested rental applications, congratulations! You're very close to having a tenant! As you make up your mind, keep Rule Two of tenant selection in mind.

Rule Two: Don't take unnecessary risks.

Don't be swayed only by someone's manner or appearance. If an application tells you in plain black and white that the applicant will be able to meet the rent only with some hardship, put the application aside and move on to another. After all, you're looking for a tenant, not a best friend, and want a tenant for whom a rent increase will not pose a burden. On the other hand, think twice about renting to someone you intensely disliked but who looks wonderful on paper—long time at job, solid income, assets that make you green with envy. Which brings us to Rules Three and Four.

Rule Three: Trust your instincts.
Rule Four: Always check references.

These two go hand in hand: no matter how much you like someone, you must always check references and, likewise, even if you have checked references you should avoid renting to someone you have a gut feeling against—too critical, too demanding, or didn't look you in the eye.

Divide your applications into three stacks. In one pile put the top two or three applications, into another the runners-up, and into another your straight rejects. Rule out anyone who doesn't meet your financial criteria (income is less than four times the rent), is unwilling to provide you with some of the information you require (leaves out name of employer) or cannot provide you with credit references (no savings or checking accounts, no credit cards, no charge accounts, no car). It's easier to eliminate potential deadbeats now than it is to go against your better judgment and take the chance of ending up in housing court three months after they move in!

A word of caution: let's say you've shown the apartment to several tenants and you have just finished talking to a woman who seems closest to your ideal tenant. You're tempted to tell her she can have the apartment right then, especially when she tells you she has seen another apartment and has to let that landlord know by the end of the day if she wants it, or when she is willing to give you a check right then and there. Don't submit to such pressure, whether or not it's deliberate. Tell her firmly but apologetically that you have to check her references and very much hope she will hold off accepting the other apartment until you have done so. This step is important—checking references is a must. Also, you should establish right from the start that you're not the kind of landlord to make decisions on the spot. Letting several hours or a day lapse, too, will make applicants just a little itchy and all the more pleased to find out, when you do finally call, that you will let them rent the apartment. However, don't delay more than a day if you can help it—your ideal tenant may not wait.

CHECKING REFERENCES

Now you're ready to check the references of your first choices. Although making the calls may seem greatly inconvenient and time-consuming, once you've done it a few times you'll have it down like clockwork and it will be a snap. Also, it's not half as time-consuming as trying to cope with bad tenants who don't pay their rent, damage your property or interfere with your enjoyment of the house.

Check references in four areas: employer, present landlord, credit references and personal references. In the course of doing so, you should always automatically rule out any applicants who have misrepresented themselves (in other words, lied) on the application. You can, if you so desire, ask a tenant to clarify any discrepancies, but chances are the applicant simply assumed that you wouldn't bother to check.

- *Employer* When you call an applicant's employer, ask to speak to the personnel department. Begin your conversation by saying, "Jim Tenant has applied to rent an apartment in my house. I would like to verify that he has worked for you for four and a half years and that his gross monthly income is two thousand dollars." You could also ask what the prospect is of Jim's continued employment there— you certainly don't want to find out that the company plans to shut down Jim's entire division, leaving Jim without a job and you without his rent check. If your tenant has job stability, it's unlikely he'll move suddenly. His job will tie him to the area and to your apartment.

- *Present landlord*   Some tenants may be reluctant to fill in this information on the application and tell you, "My landlord doesn't know I'm moving and I don't want to rock the boat until I know for sure if I have a new place to live." Don't fall for this one. Your applicants may have a good reason for not wanting their present landlord to give you an earful. Or, they may be concerned that their landlord will give *them* notice before they've found a new place to live. Firmly but politely tell such applicants that you certainly can't rent to them until you have talked with their present landlord but that you will check their other references first.

When you do call the landlord, keep in mind that you're in a bit of a sticky wicket. A landlord may give some tenants a glowing reference because he's dying to get rid of them. You can, however, ask the following questions:

— Does Jim Tenant pay the rent on time?
— Has Jim Tenant's rent check ever bounced? What were the circumstances?
— Has Jim Tenant caused any damage, however minor, to the apartment?
— Has Jim followed the rules of your house— regarding parking, pets, etc.?
— What is his monthly rent?
— How long has he lived at 12 Grove Street? (This and the previous question will determine if Jim has been truthful on his application.)
— If Jim moves out, will you be sorry to see him go?
— Is Jim being evicted?

- *Previous landlord*   Your applicant's present land-lord may be eager to have Jim move out, but Jim's *previous* landlord has nothing to lose by being honest with you. For this reason it's a good idea to make a quick call to him and ask him the same questions you've asked his present landlord.

- *Bank accounts*   You probably won't be able to verify account information by telephone, and will have to have the tenant's written permission before the bank will release any information. The day you receive the rental application, send pages 2 and 3 to the applicant's banks. If you include a self-addressed stamped envelope you should receive the verification within three days. Most banks will, however, tell you that the applicant has an account and that a check in a certain amount will clear the applicant's account. Thus you could say, "Jim Tenant is giving me a check in the amount of fifteen hundred dollars to cover rent and deposits. Will the check clear?" However, keep in mind it might clear as of that moment but not the next day when you get to the bank.

- *Credit cards and store charge cards*   If an applicant has one or more major credit or store charge cards, it indicates he or she has been considered a good risk by the business granting the card. Thus, it's a propitious sign, although there's always a chance the applicant could be overextended. However, be consoled: if Jim were to become financially strapped, he would probably pay you before Bloomingdale's—most people consider rent payment a top priority.

  As with banks, you will need written permission from your prospective applicant to obtain credit information on store charge cards and bank cards such as Master Charge or Visa.

  Rather than request credit information from individual stores, you will save time if you request it from a credit bureau. Call one of the credit references on the application and ask what credit bureau it subscribes to. That particular credit bureau probably has credit information on more than one of the applicant's accounts. Credit bureaus generally charge for this service—usually somewhere in the vicinity of twenty-five to fifty dollars for a complete report. Consider it a small price to pay for the assurance that you won't be renting to a deadbeat.

- *Personal references* Although it's a good idea to ask for personal references on the application form, don't put much—if any—stock in them. What tenant would give you the name of someone who would give a negative reference? Unless you have time or are ambivalent about the tenant after checking all the other references, don't even bother to check the personal reference. However, if you're the type that would feel more secure making one more call, by all means do so. Ask about the person's relationship to the applicant, and how long they have known each other. Then ask the reference to give you three words that best describe the applicant. Listen for words like "cooperative," "reliable," "steady," "stable." Be wary if the reference says, "A lot of fun," "Loves a party," or "Who?"

AND THE WINNER IS . . .

After you have checked the references, eliminate any applicants who have misled you. You may want to question them about any discrepancies between what they wrote on the application and what you have found out. There may be a good reason for the difference. For instance, Jim may have listed his Master Charge account balance as $125 but the credit bureau lists it as $225, reflecting a recent purchase for which he has not yet been billed. On the other hand, if he lists his rent as $400 and his landlord tells you he pays $500, his explanation had better be good! He may not want you to know he has been paying that high a rent for two years and could thus well afford your rent of $550!

Let's say your applicant's references all check out, he can

move in on the date the apartment will be available, he can provide you with a check to cover the advance money required, and he's as close as you've come to what you have in mind as the ideal tenant. You're now ready to make the call to say, "The apartment's yours." Be sure, when you do, to reiterate the terms of the tenancy: monthly rent, with or without utilities, "extras" —yard, parking—pets, etc. Ask your soon-to-be tenant to drop over with a check to clinch the deal and to sign the rental agreement containing all your policies, a copy of which you gave him when he filled out an application.

Rental Application

Name: _____

License number and make of car: _____

Address: _____

How many years at this address? _____

Reason for moving? _____

Names of people who will be living in apartment: _____
_____

(each adult must fill out an application)

Employer: _____

Address: _____ Tel. number: _____

Length of employment: _____ Occupation: _____

Gross monthly salary: _____

If employed at above less than one year,

Previous employer: _____

Address: _____ Tel. number: _____

Length of employment: _____

Gross monthly salary: _____

Other sources of income: _____
_____

Bank references:
    Checking account—Bank: _____
        Account number: _____ Balance: $_____
    Savings account—Bank: _____
        Account number: _____ Balance: $_____
    Additional accounts—Bank: _____
        Account number: _____

Credit references (name of account, account number, balance):

1. _____

2. _____

3. _____

Present landlord: _____ Tel. number: _____

Rent: $_____ Includes utilities _____

Previous landlord: _____ Tel. number: _____

Rent: $_____ Includes utilities _____

Personal reference: _____

In case of emergency, name and address of nearest living relative not living with you: _____
_____

I certify the above to be true.

_____
signature

6

⚬⚬⚬⚬

Formalizing the Agreement: Your Rights and Responsibilities

Now that you've shown the apartment to prospective tenants and found a tenant for your apartment, your job as a landlord is just beginning. You are embarking on the landlord-tenant relationship, a relationship akin to marriage in its intensity, demands and expectations. Unlike a married couple, however, you and your tenant do not necessarily share common goals—so when and if rocky times hit, there's no guarantee that your tenant will want to "work it out" or "see where you're coming from." In fact, you can almost always be sure that your tenants are only worrying about themselves most of the time, whereas you, in providing housing for someone else, have to be concerned not only with your own needs and those of others in your household but also with the needs and living conditions of your tenant, who is related to you by a contract.

A contract? But, you say, my tenant and I don't have anything as formal as a contract. In fact, you object, we don't have anything in writing. Always remember: whether your tenancy agreement is written or verbal, you have a contract with your tenant. This contract covers how much the rent is, how often and when it is paid, the duration of the tenancy, what is being rented, what the rent includes, various and sundry house rules, and the procedure either party must follow to end the tenancy. Thus, if you have told Jim Tenant, "The rent is two hundred dollars per month, payable on the first of every month, for the apartment and parking space. You can have your pet and bring your dishwasher. The only stipulation is that both of us have one rental period in which to terminate the tenancy," then you have entered into a contract with Jim that is as binding as any other legal document.

Your options as a landlord are as follows: a written lease, a written tenancy-at-will agreement, and an oral tenancy-at-will agreement. We recommend that any rental agreement be in writing, despite what your local custom dictates. It spells out what is expected and gives both parties a written record of rights and obligations. It eliminates the so-called "gray areas" and reiterates your statements about house policies. People take things more seriously if they are in writing. Also, a written contract prevents either party from using the argument, "It's your word against mine." Although an oral contract is considered legally binding, practically speaking an agreement is "only as good as the paper it's written on." If it is not written, it does not exist.

After you've decided who your tenant or tenants will be and before they move in, you should offer them a written agreement or reiterate any verbal policies. Often it's convenient to give the new tenant your agreement when you show the apartment. Suggest to your new tenants that they drop off the deposit by a certain date, sit down with them to outline any highlights of your written agreement, and ask them to review and sign it as soon as possible, but in any case tell them you would like to have it signed before they move in. This review is helpful; it gives your tenant a second look, specifies all the elements of the relationship, and alerts you immediately to any misunderstandings about the terms of the tenancy. Under no circumstances let your tenant have the key to the apartment and move in until it is signed. Some devious tenants and tenants' groups have suggested that "possession is nine tenths of the law" and advocate getting into a house before an agreement is signed, thus potentially forcing a landlord (that's you!) to take tenants to court—say, to make them pay the agreed-upon rent. Chances are you would win, but at no small financial and emotional cost. Remember, you as landlord have the final say only before you let them in the door.

THE LEASE

A lease binds you and the tenant together for a specified length of time and for specific terms; this is the primary distinguishing factor between a lease and a written or oral tenancy-at-will agreement. A lease stipulates that the rental agreement has a beginning and an end. Tradition favors a one-year lease, although it is not uncommon for a lease to last as little as four months and as long as five years. Leases can be renewed at the end of the specified period or can be "self-renewing" or "self-extending," which we don't recommend. If you intend to enter into a new lease with your tenant, why not use the end of the rental period as a good opportunity to review all the terms of the tenancy, even if you end up offering a new lease on exactly the same terms?

If you have just bought the house and the existing tenants have leases, you will be obligated, in most cases, to uphold the terms of the lease.

Despite tenants' groaning about "being tied into a lease," (which, we've discovered, is most often heard when tenants want to move prematurely or otherwise break their lease), a lease, more than the other types of rental agreements, favors the tenant. If you have a lease, you really are stuck with your tenants until the end of the term unless they violate a specific clause or clauses of the lease. Even then, because you have a lease, you have no choice but to inform tenants about their transgressions; you can then attempt to end the tenancy if they do not change. That's not to say you have to put up with a tenant who does not pay the rent as specified in the lease, but rather that you do not have the same freedom of choice that you do with a tenancy-at-will agreement. Also, if you take tenants to court over a violation of a term in the lease, you may not win unless it is substantive. If you claim your tenants are noisy, it will be your word against theirs and will probably result in some sort of compromise judgment. Also, because a lease stipulates what the rent will be for the duration of the lease, you will have no leeway if you run into some unexpected expenses.

A lease only favors a landlord's interests when the rental market is really sluggish. Then and only then will the security of knowing you have your apartment rented for a full year (or whatever the term) be worth it.

Frequently, tenants to whom you show your apartment may ask for a lease; perhaps they're on fixed incomes or some such. We recommend, if you do offer your new tenant a lease, that you offer it on a trial period first—say, for four months, after which it could be renewed for another four months or rewritten as a one-year lease.

TENANT AT WILL

A tenant-at-will agreement can be verbal or written. The former is not recommended even though it is widely used in owner-occupied two- and three-family houses. Unfortunately, it works fine until there is a dispute, at which point conversations can disintegrate into acrimonious bouts of "you never mentioned that." A verbal tenant-at-will agreement usually is limited to what the rent is, when it should be paid, and what utilities are included. Other policies often aren't specified.

Like the verbal tenancy at will, a written tenancy at will offers a week-by-week or month-by-month arrangement. Often, though, it differs from a more formal lease only in its duration— that is, it is month-by-month and not for a longer term. A tenancy-at-will agreement can be just as specific as a lease agreement in outlining rights and responsibilities.

However, the tenancy at will is in force only as long as either you or the tenant "will" it. You may, with proper notice, increase the rent or terminate or otherwise change the tenancy terms. Think of it as a "tenancy at *my* will." Your tenant, by the same token, can give notice to terminate at his or her "will." Notice of termination for a monthly tenancy must be given thirty days or one full rental period in advance, whichever is longer. Notice of termination must be written, even if your agreement is verbal.

DEPOSIT MONEY

When you collect deposit money, don't feel sorry for your tenant and wonder if the amount would pose a financial hardship. Don't follow the wisdom of local custom which dictates not collecting any deposit money. *You should get as much money in advance as the law allows, because of the risk to you and your house.* Even the maximum does not come close to equaling the amount of your risk. Your risk is the same whether or not the tenant gives you no deposit money or the maximum amount.

What are the risks? Nonpayment of rent, accidental damage, malicious damage, lack of notice before moving—any of which could easily cost you more than the amount of the deposit money.

You should check for the pertinent laws in your state to find out what you are entitled to collect at the beginning of the tenancy. In most states, you can collect in advance:

• first month's rent
• last month's rent
• security deposit
• key and lock deposit
• pet deposit

If your tenants balk at what may seem to them like large sums, explain that the cost of repairs for damage can be high and that this has always been your policy. If applicable, you could cite several personal experiences that make you as firm as you are about advance money—e.g., "We had a tenant who took all the built-in bookshelves when he moved," or whatever. This makes your new tenants less inclined to think your policy is directed at them personally. A large financial commitment will engender in your tenants a healthy respect for the house and for its policies.

If the amount of advance money poses an extreme economic hardship, you could offer to spread the security deposit and the last month's rent over two months, so that by the end of two months you would have all that is required. (You should, of course, have at least the first month's rent when the tenancy begins!) Under no circumstances collect less than the maximum.

First month's rent. Once you and the tenant have agreed on the rental, you shouldn't hold the apartment for the tenant or take it off the market until you have at least one month's rent. Let's say your apartment is available the first of September and your tenant views it on the third of August. Don't wait until the first of September to collect the first month's rent—both of you run the risk of a change of heart.

When you receive the first month's rent to hold the apartment, give your tenant a receipt (see example). Receipts should be nonrefundable in case tenants change their mind at the last minute, when you may have taken the apartment off the market and perhaps even turned away other applicants. If you were to start the process all over again in the event of a cancellation, you would lose at least a month's rent. There's nothing unfair about this; your tenants would not want to find themselves out of the apartment if the shoe were on the other foot! It's especially important for you to get a nonrefundable deposit if the tenancy is not to begin for a month or more. Conceivably, your tenant could keep looking for an apartment and reject yours only when the search was successful. Your rental agreement is a binding contract; your stipulating a nonrefundable deposit shows your tenant that you take it seriously and also gives your tenant peace of mind by ensuring that you are not going to have a change of heart either. However, you should find out if this is legal in your community.

RECEIPT OF DEPOSIT MONEY

August 3, 1985

To: Jim Tenant

Dear Jim,

I am in receipt of your check # _357_ in the amount of
$_500_ . This check is a nonrefundable deposit to hold Apart-
ment 2, 186 Pacific Street, Yourtown. It will be applied toward
the first month's rent of $_500_ when the tenancy commences
on September 1, 1985.

Sincerely,

Carol Landlord,
Landlord
186 Pacific Street
Yourtown

Last month's rent. Having the last month's rent payable in
advance protects you if the tenant decides to leave suddenly.
Also, while tenants may not appreciate it at the time, it frees
them from paying the last month's rent when they do decide to
move, enabling them to give another landlord deposit money
and the like.

Furthermore, if you don't collect the last month's rent in advance your tenants may be tempted to use their security deposit
(see below) as the last month's rent, leaving you with the option
of taking them to small claims court to recoup any damage that
might have been paid out of the security deposit. This can be
both time-consuming and expensive.

When you receive the last month's rent, give a receipt (see
example).

RECEIPT OF LAST MONTH'S RENT

September 1, 1985

To: Jim Tenant

Dear Jim:

I am in receipt of your check # _358_ in the amount of $ _500_ for the last month's rent at Apartment 2, 186 Pacific St., Yourtown.

Sincerely,

Carol Landlord,
Landlord
186 Pacific Street
Yourtown

Security deposit. In most states, this deposit can be equal only to one month's rent. It "secures" the apartment against damage. It is intended to be set up as a reserve account against which you can deduct the cost of damage at the end of the tenancy. If there are no adjustments, the tenant will receive the entire deposit back. It's important to remember that one month's rent is only a fraction of the value of your property. Thus, the deposit does not give your tenant carte blanche to wreck the property. Depending on your local ordinances, we recommend you set up this deposit as a separate, interest-bearing trustee account, placed beyond the claim of your creditors, including bankruptcy or foreclosure. Unless laws dictate otherwise, pay the tenant the interest due at the end of the tenancy. Since the money is a deposit held in reserve in the event of damage, you cannot mix your tenant's money with your own money. The deposit shouldn't be considered your money because it is the tenant's money held in reserve. You should give your tenant a receipt for the deposit (see example).

SECURITY DEPOSIT RECEIPT

September 1, 1985

To: Jim Tenant
    186 Pacific Street
    Yourtown

Dear Jim:

I am in receipt of your check # 892 in the amount of
$ 500 , as a security deposit for Apartment 2. It is being held
for you at Lucky Savings Bank, 73 Interest Lane, Yourtown; the
account # is 813579 and pays 5% interest annually.

Please see the attached Apartment Condition Report.

This deposit will be returned to you 30 days after termination
of the tenancy, pending deductions for:

- unpaid rent
- damage caused by you
- tax increases

Sincerely,

Carol Landlord,
Landlord
186 Pacific Street
Yourtown

Apartment condition report. In order for you to make deductions for damage or to return the deposit in full at the end of the
tenancy, you would be well advised (and in some states it's the
law) to make part of your rental agreement an Apartment Condition Report (sample attached). This report should be a room-
by-room description of the condition and contents of the apartment when the tenant moves in and should cover the condition
of walls, ceilings, floors, bathroom fixtures, plumbing and electrical outlets, in addition to any pieces of furniture that "go
with" the apartment, including draperies and window shades.
It's helpful in preparing the condition report to prepare yourself
for the worst. As you go through the apartment, make notes and
assume the most adversarial type of tenant will be living there.

Ask yourself, "What could go wrong?" Being specific now could prove economical in the long run. A few examples will show why this is important.

Let's say Jim Tenant moves out of your apartment after a year. When you go in to inspect the apartment after his departure, you notice that the fire extinguisher in the kitchen and the window shades in every room are missing. Also missing are the four brass wall sconces that graced the dining room wall. You check your Apartment Condition Report and realize that none of these items are listed as being part of the apartment even though you know they were there when Jim moved in. When Jim drops by to pick up his security deposit, you ask him if he took them by mistake. Jim replies, innocently enough, "I bought them when I moved in" or "I don't recall seeing them." What recourse would you have? Unfortunately, not much, unless you have photos that could somehow prove the items were yours. But even then it's your word against Jim's, and besides, are you going to go to small claims court over the items? The other course would be to deduct the cost of the items from Jim's security deposit; but if he contests, it's your word against his—and your Condition Report doesn't say anything about the items.

Or, let's say you inspect the apartment after Jim's departure and discover the hardwood floor has an enormous black grease or oil stain on it, two stove handles are missing, two globes in the chandelier are cracked, the front door has suspicious-looking scratches on it, and the bathroom tile has mold growing on it. When you ask Jim about these problems, he scratches his head, says he doesn't know anything about them, denies his dog could have scratched the door, and asserts that "that's the way it was when I moved in." If your condition report is not specific and detailed, you will have to pay for the needed repairs yourself. If, on the other hand, you itemize the condition and contents carefully, you will be able to deduct the cost of repairing or replacing anything outside the realm of normal wear and tear. Having an itemized report protects your tenant, too. Let's face it: if your tenant stays in the apartment for several years, neither of you is going to remember everything about the condition of the apartment.

To prepare your Apartment Condition Report, you should go

through the apartment room by room and systematically ask yourself about each component of each room. Here are some questions that will be helpful:

- Floor: What is the floor surface? Tile, hardwood, carpet, linoleum? What is the condition? If new, this should be stated. Where, if anywhere, are the worn spots or stains? Is floor surface clean?
- Doors, windows, door and window moldings: What is their overall condition? Are they painted or stained? Do they close properly? Are windows free of cracks or breaks? Is anything fastened on moldings?
- Walls: What are the walls covered with? Paint, wallpaper, paneling, exposed brick, corkboard? Tiles: Are they smooth and sound? Are there visible cracks? Peeling spots? Is grout in good condition? Are walls clean? Tears in wallpaper? Attached light fixtures?
- Heating elements: Note presence of radiators and condition of same. Are they in working order?
- Plumbing fixtures: What is included? Shower or tub? Condition of toilet, sink(s)? Are they functioning properly? Faucet adapter for spray dishwasher, aerator?
- Appliances: What is included? Dishwasher? Refrigerator? Washing machine? Dryer? Stove? Microwave? Brand name and model? Color? Brand-new? Interior and exterior clean?
- Ceiling: What is ceiling covered with? Tile? Plaster and paint? Overall condition? Smooth and sound? Are there visible cracks? Peeling spots? Stains from leaks? Is there an overhead light fixture? Functioning properly?
- Electrical outlets and light fixtures: Functioning properly?
- Cabinets and shelves: Color and number? Empty and clean?
- Furniture: Description of any furniture that goes with the apartment.

The Apartment Condition Report should be reviewed by your tenant and attached to the written agreement. Your tenant may not always agree with your assessment of the apartment; always be prepared to discuss any points of concern so that both you and your tenant feel the condition report is an accurate statement. An example of the Condition Report is shown below; the opening paragraph is required by Massachusetts law. Be sure and see if local ordinances dictate a specific format, inclusive of type size and face.

APARTMENT CONDITION REPORT

September 1, 1985

To: Jim Tenant
186 Pacific Street
Yourtown

Re: Apartment 2

This is a statement of the condition of the premises you have leased or rented. You should read it carefully in order to see if it is correct. If it is correct, you must sign it. This will show that you agree that the list is correct and complete. If it is not correct, you must attach a separate signed list of any damage which you believe exists in the premises. This statement must be returned to the lessor or his/her agent within fifteen (15) days after you receive this list or within fifteen (15) days after you move in, whichever is later. If you do not return this list within the specified time period, a court may later view your failure to return the list as your agreement that the list is complete and correct in any suit which you may bring to recover the security deposit.

The condition of the apartment is as follows:

Living room:_____

Dining room:_____

Foyer:_____

Bedroom:_____

Master bedroom:_____

Kitchen:_____

Bathroom:_____

Attic:_____

Family room:_____

_____   _____

   Signed: Jim Tenant   Signed: Carol Landlord
186 Pacific Street
Yourtown

Key and lock deposit. If you replace the existing lock with a new one before the tenant moves in, you are entitled to collect from your tenant the cost of a new lock. You may also collect from your tenant a deposit for each key you provide; this key deposit is refundable when the key is returned at the end of the tenancy. Again, check for existing statutes.

Pet deposit. Some states allow you to collect a deposit from tenants who will have pets. One landlord we know collects half a month's rent to protect him against damages a pet can cause, and the specific potential damages are itemized: flea damage, urine stains, odor, scratches and the like, depending on the kind of pet. Also, he does not return the deposit for forty-five days—as he pointed out, "Sometimes we can't determine whether there are fleas until someone else moves in."

WHEN DOES THE TENANCY BEGIN?

The tenancy should begin as soon as the apartment is available, or, as soon as the house is yours if it has tenants already. It shouldn't begin when the tenant can move in—otherwise you may lose several weeks' or a month's rent. Let's say Jim Tenant moves out the thirty-first of July but Joan Tenant doesn't have to vacate her apartment until the end of August. Joan asks if it would be all right if she moved in on the first of September. Your reply should be a standard one: "Feel free to move in whenever you want but the tenancy really has to begin as soon as the apartment is available, August 1. Other people are interested in it for that date—we simply can't lose a month's rent." Although we don't recommend compromising, you may find an ideal tenant whose circumstances don't permit immediate occupancy. In that instance, you could choose an in-between date on which to begin the tenancy; thus your tenant would, say, have the apartment two weeks earlier than she needs it and you would have it filled two weeks after it was vacated. Under no circumstances should you absorb the entire burden of accommodating yourself to someone else's schedule.

If you bought the house with tenants, you will want them to

have a written agreement with you. Review their existing agreements to be sure they include your policies. If your tenants have a lease that predates your ownership, you probably cannot rewrite it until the end of the term.

THE WRITTEN AGREEMENT

Whether you decide to go forward with a lease or a written tenancy-at-will agreement, you would do well to use a standard one, tailored to your specifications. Standard leases are available at stationery stores, real estate boards, housing boards and state housing commissions (if they aren't directly available there, the personnel can certainly tell you where to find one). However, before filling it in and having your tenant sign it, make sure *you* know what each clause means so you can answer your tenant's questions.

The advantages of using a standard lease or rental agreement are as follows: someone else has done the thinking for you; your tenant will be reassured that your agreement is widely used; agreements that are available from local or state real estate boards probably incorporate the latest laws and regulations about rent control and the like; a printed agreement gives you credibility as a professional. It's a funny thing—but if you take the time and care to draw up your own agreement from scratch (with, of course, the help of a lawyer) and type it, chances are your tenant will be wary that it contains something amiss. If you do pursue that course, have your agreement typeset and printed so that it looks standard.

Since laws protecting tenants are constantly changing, it is important that your agreement comply with the law. Check with your local housing court or an attorney to be sure all of the provisions in your lease are within the law.

WHAT SHOULD YOUR RENTAL AGREEMENT INCLUDE?

Your rental agreement should be signed by all parties and should describe in specific detail what your rights and responsibilities are and what your tenant's rights and responsibilities are. If possible, have everything in plain English and be sure to give each of your tenants a copy of the signed agreement. Whether you use a standard form lease or devise your own, be sure your agreement contains provisions for the following:

- Name, address and telephone number of landlord
- Address of premises
- Names of all legal occupants
- Description of premises: number of rooms, number of stories, heated or unheated
- The term of the agreement: e.g., one month, four months, one year
- How much the rent is, how often and where it should be paid, and what late charges may apply
- Tax escalator clause (if you have a lease, this provides for an increase in rent if your real estate taxes go up)
- If the apartment is subject to rent control or rent stabilization (if the lease is for more than one year, a provision about raising the rent should be included)
- Heat and utilities: who pays for what (if your tenant pays for heat, consider adding a line about keeping heat at a minimum setting of 60°)
- Keys and locks (this stipulates that the tenant may not change the locks and that the landlord must repair or replace broken locks)
- Cleanliness and care of the dwelling
- Use of and maintenance of common areas and grounds
- Parking
- Pets
- Water beds
- Proper use of plumbing
- Subletting and/or new occupants
- Amount of security deposit

- Alterations and improvements, including any promises you are making
- Maintenance of the unit
- Right of entry to make repairs, inspect the unit, or show the apartment to prospective tenants or buyers
- Restriction of illegal or business activity
- Rules and regulations
- Termination or renewal of agreement
- Installation of fixtures
- Nonperformance on the part of the tenant (nonpayment of rent, violation of terms of the lease)

You will also want to include specific provisos related to the apartment. As one thorough urban landlord told us, "Rules of contract are only limited by the human imagination. My agreements could be three hundred pages if I wanted." Don't be afraid to be as specific as you want. If you have more than one apartment, keep the major provisions the same while tailoring each agreement to the apartment in question.

To further underline what exactly the terms of your agreement are, you might want to summarize at the bottom: "This agreement constitutes the entire agreement between Jim Tenant and Carol Landlord. No promises have been made that do not appear herein."

As your tenancy progresses, make a note about any addenda that should be incorporated into a new lease or as part of the tenancy-at-will agreement. If you have a tenancy at will, you certainly don't want to be amending the agreement every month to cover minor revisions; accumulate enough of them to make it worth your while.

LANDLORD'S RESPONSIBILITIES

The rental agreement should spell out your precise responsibilities. Your responsibilities in the agreement should correspond to your local and state laws. You may never get into hot water by doing more than you are required, but you certainly can by doing less! Make it your business—since it *is* your business—to know what the building and housing codes say, to know what the landlord-tenant laws in your state are, and to know not only what is required but what the penalties are for noncompliance or nonperformance. Ignorance may be bliss until you discover—the hard way—that you have violated various laws and are being sued by your tenant for damages. As the head of a state tenants' association told us, "Large professional landlords know the law; small landlords find out in court." Familiarize yourself with your responsibilities vis-à-vis the physical premises and vis-à-vis the occupants. Although you may wish to assign some of your responsibilities to your tenants, don't do it—even if they consent.

Remember, you may not have a financial choice about how to spend your money if your responsibilities as a landlord so dictate. If your tenant's furnace goes, you cannot "live with it" for several weeks, as you might do in your own part of the house. Your responsibilities require you to be *more* responsive than you would be to your own standards. You have to be concerned with a third party—the state or local municipality which dictates your responsibilities.

The general "concept" of being a landlord has changed over the past twenty years; the landlord is not simply the person with the "land" who provides space to those who have no land of their own. Rather, rental housing has become a consumer service and has come—in many states—under the protection of the law. Its being looked at as a consumer service has resulted in an "implied warrant of habitability"; that is, any rental unit has to conform to minimum property standards requirements. Gone are the days when a landlord can knowingly rent an apartment without a toilet or a bathroom—and get away with it. In days past, landlords could shrug their shoulders and sigh and say, "Well, you saw it that way and now you're stuck with it," or "What do you expect for a hundred dollars a month?" Often now the tenant is protected from such deception. Apartments have to conform to certain standards; it's not enough to have a tenant willing to put up with unhealthy conditions.

It's your responsibility to know what is required by law. You're responsible for delivering an apartment that is habitable and therefore have to know how "habitable" is defined. Not only are you carrying the burden of providing housing but you are also responsible for making sure you are in compliance with state codes. Don't be swayed by friends and associates who tell you to be casual or not to worry, or even by your tenants' seeming satisfaction with the way things are. Make it your business to find out.

The first thing we recommend is to have your house and all of its apartments inspected by either an independent or a municipal housing inspector to ascertain its condition and any steps required to make the apartments comply with the building and sanitary code. If you have just bought the house, chances are you already had this done.

Chances are, if you act reasonably and responsibly, you will conform to any codes. Consumer protection laws, however, are designed to protect your tenant. For example, you are required to provide secure locks on interior and exterior doors (in fact, some state codes are specific enough to require a landlord to have an exterior door that closes automatically). If your tenant is robbed after someone breaks down the door, you have still acted reasonably. If, on the other hand, you neglected to repair a broken lock, you may be liable for the tenant's losses.

Next, contact your state housing authority, attorney general's office, local housing court or commission, zoning boards, health and sanitation department, rent control board, building department and tenants' groups to gather as much information as possible about what the laws are in your state and locality. Many of these will have publications available for purchase or free. Probably your most valuable documents will be copies of the "health and sanitary code" and "building code." These will tell you about room sizes, what is required, what has to be in working order. Take the time to read through them—they will detail how big a room has to be to be called a bedroom, where smoke detectors are required, if lead paint is prohibited, what to do about insects, and the like. It will also inform you how soon you must make repairs (e.g., within two weeks of receipt of notice of disrepair). If there are seminars on landlording, tenants' rights or housing issues—often available at adult education centers—sign up!

Make sure you know what the laws are regarding discrimination. These may not seem to be directly tied in with the condition of your house, but they can be. For example, in Massachusetts, it is illegal to refuse to rent to someone with children. It is also illegal to have lead paint in an apartment with children under six. What do you do when you find out your entire house has lead paint? Does this give you the right to discriminate? No! You must have the premises "deleaded." But be sure to have the deleading done by a professional who is prepared to deal with the resultant fumes and who also can delead without damaging the apartment and its character.

In addition to knowing what is required in terms of the physical condition of the apartment, find out about your responsibilities in performing as a landlord. If you want to terminate the tenancy, how much notice do you have to give? Do you have "right of entry"? What are your rights if your tenant stops paying the rent? Your best source for this information is your local housing court. Ask if they have any free literature for interested parties. Another way of finding out what the laws are is to contact local tenants' groups, especially since they often focus on abuses and means of redress. Also, they often have literature that will alert you to potential problems. Smart landlords are members of both tenants' and landlords' organizations.

In general, your responsibilities (according to the U.S. Department of Housing) can be summarized as follows:

- Comply with the requirements of applicable building and housing codes materially affecting health and safety;
- Make all repairs and do whatever is necessary to put and keep the premises in a fit and habitable condition;
- Keep all common areas of the premises in a clean, safe, sanitary and livable condition (this is the "warranty of habitability");
- Maintain in good and safe working order and condition all safety features, including locks and intercoms, electrical, plumbing, sanitary, heating, ventilating, air-conditioning and

other facilities and appliances, including elevators supplied or
required to be supplied by the landlord;
- Provide and maintain appropriate receptacles and conve-
niences for the removal of ashes, garbage, rubbish and other
waste incidental to the occupancy of the dwelling unit, and
arrange for their removal;
- Supply running water and reasonable amounts of hot water at
all times and reasonable heat, usually between October 1 and
May 1, except where the tenant has complete control over the
heating system and pays the bill to a public utility or a private
company;
- Provide for the quiet enjoyment of the premises by the tenant;
this includes privacy, peace, quiet, and use of the premises;
- May not charge rent in excess of any legal limits.

LANDLORD'S RIGHTS

Since you may now feel as though through the forest of responsibility you cannot see the trees of rights and benefits, we
would like to summarize what your rights are as a landlord:
- You have the right to choose the tenant most qualified for the
unit;
- You have the right to collect a deposit against potential damage in addition to other sums;
- You have the right to be paid rent, on time and in full;
- You have the right of entry or access to make repairs or improvements, to provide agreed-on services, to correct an emergency or inspect the apartment, and to show the apartment to
prospective workers, contractors, lenders, and purchasers, as
well as if the premises appear to be abandoned (however, you
should try to arrange a mutually convenient time);
- You have the right to evict a tenant or otherwise terminate the
tenancy for nonpayment of rent, for violations of the lease, to
transfer ownership, to allow someone from your immediate
family to move in, or, in the case of a tenancy at will, because
you no longer wish to continue with the tenancy;

- You have the right to receive the apartment back in its original condition, reasonable wear and tear excepted.

TENANT'S RESPONSIBILITIES

Your tenant has certain responsibilities which should be stated in the rental agreement. Remember, you cannot assign your tenant some of the responsibilities that are legally yours, such as shoveling the walks or keeping the common area clean.

Your tenant has to maintain the apartment in a clean and orderly fashion and has to dispose of rubbish, trash and garbage in a safe and sanitary manner. Many standard leases stipulate that tenants cannot throw trash and garbage out the windows or doors; if you follow our earlier suggestions for tenant screening, you won't have to enforce that caveat!

Your tenant has to use all aspects of the physical plant of the apartment—that is, electrical, plumbing and heating systems—in a safe and appropriate manner.

Your tenant cannot deface, damage or remove any of the premises! Your tenant cannot abuse the premises.

Your tenant may use the house and grounds only for residential use and may not engage in business or commercial activity, unless you agreed to this in advance.

Your tenant has to deliver the premises in good and clean condition at the end of the tenancy.

Your tenant cannot be excessively noisy.

Your tenant is responsible for making or paying for repairs for damage he or she caused.

TENANT'S RIGHTS

Your tenant has a number of rights, and their number is growing, due in large part to increasing protections tenants receive under the law. Many of their rights are the flip side of your responsibilities; for example, your tenant has the right to live in a space that conforms to the sanitary code and you are obligated to maintain your apartment according to the code.

Your tenant's rent is paid in exchange for a "warrant of habitability."

Your tenant has the right to privacy and "quiet enjoyment," a legal term that means your tenant should not be prevented from using and occupying the apartment.

Your tenant has the right to be given proper notice when you want to gain access to the apartment, except during an emergency.

Your tenant has the right to report violations or suspected violations to the local building or health department, although the landlord has the right to be informed of these before any report to an inspector.

Your tenant has the right to organize other tenants to press you for better or improved services if you haven't responded to written requests, as well as the right to join a tenants' group.

Your tenant may have the right to withhold rent under certain conditions or to "repair and deduct" for necessary repairs. But again, the tenant has to give the landlord prior written reasonable notice of problems that exist before resorting to these forms of redress.

You should familiarize yourself with what the "hot issues" are among local tenants.

It is a two-way street. Landlords deserve the same measure of respect implied in giving and in receiving proper written notice of anything that would materially affect them.

7

The Ground Rules

Your tenant signs the lease or tenancy agreement and moves in. The night before trash day, Jim Tenant puts out his trash in paper bags. The numerous neighborhood dogs don't waste a minute and have a grand time with the porkchop bones and chicken carcasses; they leave a greasy mess behind, strewing garbage and trash everywhere in front of your house. That evening you knock on the door and explain you would like the trash in plastic bags on trash day.

The following weekend you haul three bags of laundry downstairs to the laundry area. Your tenant has beaten you to it—the machines are churning and your tenant has left two additional loads next to the machines. It will be hours before his wash is done. You're especially irritated because you need to wear your brown pants tonight and you're going to be out all afternoon. You wish you had thought through your tenant's use of the laundry room and considered instituting a policy whereby your tenant could use the area only on weekdays.

The next evening, just as you're turning off the eleven o'clock news, you hear what sounds like a jet engine but is more likely a vacuum cleaner roaring above you. You just can't believe anyone would want to clean house at that hour and curse your naïveté for assuming that people keep hours similar to yours. After ten minutes of fuming, you pick up the phone and read your new tenant the riot act.

Thus, by the end of only the first week, you and your new

tenant are just short of declaring war. Your tenant is on edge, sure that you'll knock on the door any minute; you're vigilant, sure that your tenant is going to violate one of your unspoken rules.

Sound familiar? Do you feel you're always on your tenants' back about something and on the lookout to make sure your tenants do things "your way"? You can't assume that your tenants will follow your example and learn by osmosis, nor can you assume that they will have the foresight to ask how things should be done.

The solution? Just as a Yankee innkeeper posts the rules about checkout time and fees on the guest's door, so should you have a definite house policy. Decide the rules of the house before any tenant moves in. Explain the policies while you are showing the apartment and have them available in writing to be part of the lease or written tenancy agreement. Find out in advance if your tenants understand the various rules and are willing to follow them while living in your house. Tell your tenants, and make it part of your written agreement, that their failure to comply will be just cause for you to send them a notice to quit the apartment. This will indicate to your tenants that you mean business. And don't be afraid to follow through should the time come. Also, at the end of your written list, be sure to add: "Anything not specifically contained herein shall not constitute permission."

Specific ground rules are second only to the choice of a tenant for establishing a successful landlord-tenant relationship. It is far better to be direct in advance about your expectations than to "wait and see how things go" or to be unhappy about the way something is done.

Your tenants do have a right to privacy and the right to the quiet enjoyment of their apartment. If you don't set the rules early on, you will be in the position of constantly intruding on the tenants' peace and quiet. They will wonder when you'll strike next. This creates resentment and bad feelings all around. You will put the tenants on the defensive by making them feel they're doing everything wrong. Also, your assertiveness will continually remind them that you are the one in power in the relationship since you are the one to tell them what to do. No one likes to be told what to do too often, and your tenants are no exception. Likewise, no one likes to be reminded that one doesn't have any power! Contrary to common misconceptions, your tenants do want to make you happy.

Further, when you go over the ground rules with your tenants, you let them know in a subtle but definite way who is the boss. Your rights and their rights are not equal—tenants cannot decide how things will be done. You as the landlord and only you have that privilege. If you provide tenants with a written list of house policies right at the beginning of the tenancy, you establish right away that things will be done *your* way. And, you won't be in a position to have to keep reestablishing it (unless your tenants fail to comply).

Finally, by explaining the house policies at the beginning of the tenancy, you will make a good impression on your tenants. They'll appreciate your having taken the time to think things through and will respect you for your honesty and directness. You'll both know where you stand and will be off to a good start.

What are some of the elements of a sound house policy and how should you begin to formulate it? If you have never had a tenant, you can get some ideas from the rest of this chapter, which will itemize what some of the common areas of concern are. Basically, you should try to anticipate what your tenant's needs are and how these fit in with how you want things done. Likewise, you'll have to think about your own desires—which you've already done if you have followed the suggestions in Chapter 1. For example, if this is your first house and yard, you may know right now that you don't want your tenant using the yard. Make it part of your policy. It's a lot easier to restrict tenants at the beginning than to do so later or to limit their use of the yard to times when you are not home.

If you have had a series of tenants, you know some of the things that you wish had been done differently. Now's the time to remember all of them and make them part of your house policy. If Joe's stereo bothered you, chances are any new tenant's loud stereo will also bother you. Don't be afraid to cite previous tenants' transgressions—specific examples give credibility to your policies.

There are four areas you should give some thought to: business, privacy, use and abuse, and possessions.

Your relationship with your tenant is first and foremost a business relationship. Your tenant pays you a monthly rent in exchange for the use of the space. If the business end of the relationship is not going smoothly, it isn't going to make any difference how clean or quiet your tenant is. Thus, you should formulate a rent payment policy, some ideas for which follow below.

Your house policy should also protect your privacy and that of your tenants. This doesn't mean you should ask people to sneak around, not to peep through your windows or eavesdrop outside your door. That would be paranoid of you! However, as Robert Frost so aptly put it, "Good fences make good neighbors." You should anticipate how you and your tenant can coexist without each being constantly reminded of the other's presence. In other words, you don't want to hear the tenant or see the tenant too much. You probably don't want to smell the tenant either! Your house policy should reflect your desire to maximize your own and your tenant's privacy.

You should also give your tenants specific guidelines about how you expect your house will be used. Be clear about the use of your possessions, such as lawn furniture, snow shovels and the like. By the same token, you should announce defined strictures against abuse or damage of your house. While you can expect a certain amount of wear and tear, let your tenants know they should plan to leave their apartment as they found it, and that you will penalize them for doing otherwise.

Following are a number of areas to think about as you draw up your personal list of ground rules. This list covers areas of concern common to many landlords but may not be relevant to the idiosyncracies of your building or unit.

TERM OF TENANCY

If you have a lease or written tenancy-at-will agreement, your written agreement will specify the duration of the tenancy, whether it is a year, a month or a week. If you have a verbal tenancy-at-will agreement, be sure you tell your tenant that it is a month-to-month tenancy (or however long you wish)—in other words, that either party has to give a full month's notice before ending the tenancy.

RENT PAYMENT

If there's one thing all landlords look forward to, it's the day the rent is due. And, if there's anything they get anxious about, it's when the day comes and goes and the rent hasn't been paid. They wonder how they'll cope with the incoming bills if tenants are several weeks late in their payments, if they have lost their job or are planning to move out in the middle of the night, and further, how and when a tenant should be confronted about the problem. Perhaps he—the landlord—was foolhardy enough to have spent the money before he received it. But what if the rent never gets paid? The landlord panics! He retraces the tenant's payment history and he realizes that for the past six months the tenant has paid erratically—two days early last month, on the third of the month several times, on the first once, and so on. The landlord could have saved himself a lot of worry if he had set out a rent payment policy right at the beginning of the tenancy.

Unless you have an overriding reason to do otherwise, it's sensible to have the rent due on the first of the month. This is standard practice and most tenants are used to paying on the first—they're conditioned to this date. Also, unless you want to spend the evening of the first waiting for the tenant to appear with the rent, you can take it one step further and request that the rent be paid by, say, 9 A.M. on the first. That will enable you to use the money on the first or to take it to the bank that day. After all, your tenant has the use of the apartment on the first—

why shouldn't you have the use of the money on the first? Likewise, you may want to ask to have the rent check by 7 P.M.—and thereby save yourself the anxiety that accompanies watching the clock on the evening of the first.

When you specify the day the rent must be paid, you will also know early if there is a problem, instead of wondering if the tenant is just a bit absent-minded or in financial trouble. Also, you will not surprise your tenants if you knock on their door asking for the rent if they fail to pay by the appointed time on the appointed day.

You should also specify that the rent must be paid by that time even if your tenant will be away that day. More tenants have returned home to an angry landlord after a three-day weekend than you can shake a stick at. Let your tenants know that if they plan to be away they will have the choice of paying you before they leave or sending you the rent. After all, you're as close as a twenty-two-cent stamp!

Let your tenant know how you want to be paid, whether by check or money order or cashier's check. It's a good idea to request the first month's rent and any advance money in the form of a cashier's check or money order, so that you don't find out after you've deposited a tenant's personal check that it bounced. On the other hand, this may alienate your new tenant from you. A more humane course would be to accept a personal check but tell your tenant that you are in the habit of cashing the rent checks on the first. That way, the tenant will be sure to have enough money in the account that day and not rely on a week's worth of bank float time. Don't, repeat don't, let your tenants pay you in cash. If they're robbed on the way home, they're probably going to be unable to pay the rent. And if you're robbed on the way to the bank, you're going to lose a month's rent.

Let your tenants know to whom the check or money order should be made out, whether to you personally, to your spouse, or to the name of your business if you have the building set up as a trust. This sounds like an obvious thing to tell a tenant, but it's a detail many landlords forget. One husband-and-wife team was forever frustrated because their tenant always wrote the check out to the husband, but the wife was the one who did the banking. They were reluctant to tell the tenant to do otherwise for fear the tenant would think less of the husband for seemingly not controlling the purse-strings.

If your tenants are unrelated (three women, say), specify if you want to receive one check or three. Three checks would have to clear your bank. Also, receiving three checks dilutes the responsibility—if one tenant is away, the rent can't be paid in full.

Let your tenants know if they should expect a receipt or if their canceled check is their receipt. To be absolutely correct, you should give your tenant a receipt for each month's rent. But if you feel you already are drowning in paperwork, use the canceled check and even suggest that your tenant write on the check the month it covers.

Let the tenant know as you explain your rent policy how the rent will be collected. Decide in advance if you want to collect it personally or have the tenant deliver it to you. There are advantages and disadvantages to each method of collection. If you collect it personally, you will have a chance to survey the apartment (albeit from the doorway!) and to ask if the tenant has any problems, which you can look at right then and there. Your monthly visit will, you hope, motivate your tenant to keep the apartment tidy. On the other hand, if your tenant delivers the rent on the first, it doesn't necessarily mean that you have to be home to receive it—he or she could leave it under the door or in your mailbox, if you are away. Also, you won't be put on the spot to inspect any problems—you can tell the tenant you will stop by tomorrow or over the weekend. By putting the responsibility on your tenants to pay on time, you give them the feeling that you trust them and don't have to invade their privacy on the first. They will appreciate not having to be home when you are expected to come by. However you decide to collect the rent, be consistent with all of your tenants.

Finally, stress to your tenants as you explain your rent payment policies that you want to know as soon as possible if they will have a problem paying the rent. Be understanding as you say this—"I know every once in a while an emergency arises that may leave you strapped financially and may make you late with the rent. If that happens, please let me know as soon as possible so we can plan how you'll pay." Be firm at the same time, by concluding, "Naturally, we don't expect this to happen on any kind of a regular basis, but we did want you to know that we want you to tell us as soon as you know there will be a problem." However, don't make this part of your written ground rules—it might encourage tenants to get into the habit of not paying on time.

Some landlords make it a policy to assess a late charge if the tenant is late more than a specified number of days. This is not a bad idea but is not legal in some areas, so check with your local housing authority before you institute it.

TRASH AND GARBAGE COLLECTION

Don't wait for your tenants to ask how the trash should be disposed of—let them know what your expectations are.

If you have trash collection, tell your tenants what day trash is collected and when they should put it out. If you neglect to tell them *when,* they may put it out the night before and it will attract the local dogs! Tell them if you have garbage cans available, if you want them to use plastic garbage bags, and where their trash should be stored—basement, garage, or their own apartment—between collections. If they do store it in a public part of the house, be clear about whose responsibility it will be—yours or theirs—to take it out to the street. If the tenants are to be responsible, avoid confusion and buy one or two fifty-gallon covered trash cans for each unit. Label them Apartment 1, Apartment 2, etc.

If you have no trash collection, tell your tenants what the dump hours are and any particulars about the dump. For instance, some dumps require that bottles and cans be separated from other garbage. Tell your tenants that you expect them to go to the dump on a weekly basis and make that part of your agreement. You certainly don't want your house smelling like two-week-old garbage. Depending on your inclination you may find it easier to take the trash to the dump yourself, especially if you would rather be sure it gets done or if you have a tenant who lacks a car or for whom a trip to the dump would pose a handicap.

PARKING

Dealing with parking is easy only when your tenants don't have a car. Otherwise, it involves some thought. You can make it easy on yourself if you think through carefully what your own needs are, what space you have available, and whether or not to let your tenants use it.

If you have as many spaces as you do apartments in your house, be sure to assign a space to each apartment and to let your tenants know which space is theirs. Specify if the parking space is included in the monthly rent or if it is extra.

If you have fewer spaces than you do apartments, assign the spaces on a first-come, first-served basis unless there is a reason to do otherwise; for instance, if the only available space is adjacent to the first-floor apartment, then it makes sense to have the space permanently assigned to that apartment.

If you have more spaces than you do apartments, consider yourself lucky! If your tenants need more than one space, they should be willing to pay extra for a second space. After all, you would probably be able to rent the space to someone else. In any case, make its status clear—don't leave it up for grabs.

If you don't have any parking spaces for your tenants, let them know if street parking is permitted. At the same time, let them know if the street has "implied assigned spaces." In some communities, if you park in front of Mr. Jones' house, you make him your enemy for life! You also will want to let your tenants know where they might rent a space. If yours is a neighborhood where parking spaces are at a premium, always keep your ears to the ground about possible rental spaces.

Be sure to let your tenants know where guests may park. You certainly don't want them parking in your space or in front of Mr. Jones' house. If in front of the house is okay, say so. Likewise, if the metered space down by the corner is all that's usually free, again, tell them.

PETS

Tenants must know your pet policy in advance, regardless of whether or not they had a pet when they applied for the apartment. Let's say Jim Smith rents your apartment. Six months later you hear some kind of small animal running around upstairs and discover that Jim has a new kitten. When you tell Jim he has to get rid of the kitten which is extremely cute, he argues, saying that he had no idea you didn't allow pets, asking why you didn't tell him that was the case. It's difficult under those circumstances to make Jim get rid of the kitten, even more so because you know he's right—you should have let him know what your policy is.

Just as important as letting your tenants know your policy— be consistent with all of your tenants. You can't let the people in Apartment 1 have a pet if the people in Apartments 2 and 3 can't have one. The only exception to this is the case of a tenant with a seeing-eye dog. A second exception may have to be made for tenants who predate you in the building: that is, if you bought the building with existing tenants and their existing pets. If that's the case, you should make it clear to those tenants that only their existing pets are allowed; no new pets can be brought to live in your house.

With these two caveats in mind, formulate your pet policy. Keep in mind that pets can cause significant damage to floors, carpets, draperies and walls. Always require a security deposit from a tenant whom you allow to have a pet. Also keep in mind that any responsible tenants are probably responsible pet owners and may be willing to pay a premium to keep their pets. In other words, if you allow a pet, you can probably charge a bit more for the privilege.

Tell your tenants what types of pets are permitted: fish, caged pets (hamsters, gerbils, mice, birds), cats, dogs, snakes or exotic pets. No matter what you allow, stress that you must give your prior approval before any pet is allowed in the house. Otherwise, your tenants may want to raise an entire litter of kittens. After all, they might argue, "You did say cats were permitted."

Don't be afraid to require certain things of the pets and their owners. For example:

• If you allow cats, you will want to know if the cat will go outdoors or not. You'd be well advised to allow only declawed indoor cats which can't damage your floors or carpets with their claws. Outdoor cats can wreak havoc with your flower beds. Also, they are more susceptible to diseases such as feline leukemia and are more likely to harbor fleas, ticks and worms. Make it a policy to allow only neutered cats. Tomcats may spray all over the apartment; the odor is quite strong and hard to remove from woodwork and carpets. Female cats go into heat, attract any male cat within five miles, and have litters. Speaking of litter, tell your tenants the litter box must be kept in the kitchen, bathroom or any other room with a linoleum floor and tell them you want them to use Litter Green or newspaper in it rather than the clay-type litter, which gets tracked through the house, scratches the wood floors, and can clog up the plumbing when the box is washed. Tell the tenants you expect the box to be changed frequently, too.

• If you allow dogs, it goes without saying that the dog must be housebroken—but say it anyway. To be absolutely safe, you may want to prohibit puppies unless a tenant is home all day to look after one. Thus you could allow tenants who already have adult dogs, but specify that they can't get a puppy at any time after moving in. Specify that dogs must be neutered, especially if the dog is a female, for the reasons cited above. Also, allow only licensed dogs which have had all their shots. Ask to see the license and a certificate of immunization from the veterinarian. Make it clear that you will not tolerate excessive barking, that is to say, you don't want to hear the dog barking for long periods. If it hears someone at the door that's one thing, but it shouldn't bark for two hours after your tenant leaves the house. Be firm about this, and add that you'll require the dog to be muzzled if your policy is violated. (Incidentally, muzzling is not painful or upsetting to the dogs themselves.)

Depending on your preference and any applicable city ordinances, you may want to specify that a dog must be kept on a leash whenever it goes out, that the tenant pick up its messes, and that the dog be kept out of your yard and out of public areas of your property.

Tell your tenants that dogs can't be left alone overnight and that if they intend to be away they must take their dog to a kennel or someone's house; don't encourage your tenants to ask friends to come in to walk the dog—it's too much of a risk for house security.

Finally, before renting to dog owners, don't settle for the owners' description of their beloved pooch. *Meet the dog.* Always. Otherwise you may end up with a yapper or a vicious dog living in your house.

• If you allow caged animals, put a limit on how many gerbils or hamsters are allowed. Three of any small animal is plenty!

• If you allow exotic pets, such as monkeys (no kidding!), be sure to request a certificate of immunization from a veterinarian.

If you decide to allow pets it's a good idea to specify that the first thirty days the tenant has a pet are considered a trial period and that you will inspect the apartment during that time to ascertain that the pet has not caused any damage. Convey that any damage caused by the pet or infraction of your pet policy shall be just cause for you to give the tenant notice to quit or to get rid of the pet within forty-eight hours. Further, let your tenants know that if they get a pet without your approval they will have to get rid of it within forty-eight hours, no matter if it is a pet you allow or not. Tell your tenants you've had to take the cutest dogs to the pound because previous tenants didn't follow your policy.

NOISE

All of the occupants of your house are entitled to the quiet enjoyment of their apartments. If your tenants make excessive noise on a regular or even an occasional basis they disrupt and violate your peace and quiet. While you probably hope to avoid renting to someone who socializes every night in the week until 3 A.M. and likes to end the week with a bang, you will do well to let your tenants know what your noise policy is, and to follow it yourself.

• Stereo and television. Tell your tenants you would like them to play their stereo and television at reasonable volume only until 11 P.M. Ask them if this would be a problem.

• Musical instruments. Tell your tenants you permit musical instruments with your prior approval—soothing piano music drifting in from their apartment is a far cry from drumbeats, the eerie tones of a Moog synthesizer, or the rousing cry of a trombone. If your tenants will be at home when no one else will be in the house, they could be asked to play their instrument during that time. Otherwise, depending on the type of instrument, you would restrict the hours of use. For instance, they would be allowed to play drums from 7 to 8 P.M., Monday through Thursday, or to play the piano from 7 to 10 P.M. daily. Reserve the right to set greater limits once the tenants have moved in and given you the opportunity to hear for yourself.

• Appliances. Ask your tenants to use major appliances— dishwasher, washing machine, vacuum cleaner—before 11 P.M. so that you're not kept awake. We developed this policy quickly when we discovered our new tenant battled her insomnia by vacuuming: apparently it wore her out or soothed her nerves. She had the most dust-free apartment in the building for several nights in a row while we walked around bleary-eyed!

• Car repair. Tell your tenants you don't expect them to tune up their car on a weekly basis. The accompanying revving-up of the engine will otherwise drive you bananas!

• Closing doors. Ask your tenants to close doors gently. This may seem obvious, but experience has shown us that some tenants don't know how to close doors. The constant slamming of doors—both outer and inner doors—is both startling and noisy, to say nothing of the damage to the door or your nerves.

• Parties. You don't want to be a party-pooper, but you really should have a policy for parties. Otherwise your tenants will have parties that annoy you in some way and you will feel compelled to announce your party policy the morning after. Your party policy should have at least three ingredients. First, tell your tenants you want to be notified of an upcoming party of more than ten people at least a week in advance. This may cramp some tenants' style—they can't spontaneously decide to ask everyone back to their house after a game or whatever—but if they know the policy in advance they'll have to live with it.

It's a good idea to suggest a limit on the number of guests. This will discourage your tenants from having a free-for-all open house.

Third, give your tenants an ending hour for any parties. This doesn't mean that all the guests have to leave by your appointed time, but that you won't be able to hear them after that hour: 2 or 3 A.M. is not unreasonable. You and your other tenants don't want to be awakened by guests slamming doors as they leave (especially since the guests don't know your door policy!). One tenant of ours told us he liked this policy because it enabled him to ask his guests to leave when the appointed hour rolled around, and he could blame his landlord. If you're invited to a tenant's party, by all means go for a drink but be sure to leave well before the ending hour approaches!

You may also want to be clear about setting a limit on the number of parties you'll permit. Four per year is a reasonable number—it's not too strict but allows one a season.

Be sure to tell your tenants about any other restrictions. For instance, if you don't permit dance parties that will shake your chandelier or barbeques on the porch that will smoke up your living room, tell your tenants up front. Don't assume that your tenants are going to be as refined as you are. One landlord we know sat beneath her living room chandelier for three hours and watched it rock back and forth as her tenant and his guests danced the night away! Her ceiling developed a hairline crack as a result—and it could have been avoided!

SAFETY AND SECURITY

Convey to your tenants that you take the safety of the building's occupants and the security of the building very seriously, that you will not tolerate any action that jeopardizes them, and that you will send a notice to quit for any infractions. And do it!

• Doors and keys. Make it a ground rule that doors have to be locked at all times. Even if they are just running down to the corner mailbox, tenants should lock their own door and the building's front door. Further, garages, bulkheads and basement doors have to be kept locked.

Tell your tenants that you do not permit keys to be lent on a regular basis under any circumstances. If your tenants are going to be away for an extended period and need their fish fed, volunteer to do it yourself. Naturally, if a tenant's mother is in town, it's entirely different from a tenant's friends dropping over.

Tell your tenants that you do not permit keys to be duplicated either, and that keys are for the occupants only. You don't, of course, want to be unreasonable or interfere with a steady romance. Thus, if asked, you could allow a tenant's girl friend to have a key. However, be sure to get the key back if they break up!

Tell your tenants you want to know immediately if their keys are lost so you can change the locks and give them a new set.

• Windows. Tell your first-floor tenants that the ground-floor windows should be kept locked when they are out. Even better, install window locks so that the windows can't be opened more than two inches. These are available at any hardware store.

• Stairways and hallways. Specify that these have to be kept lighted and clear for passage.

• Electrical matters. Don't allow your tenants to use extension cords for anything but lamps, clocks and stereos. Air conditioners and appliances will overload the circuit and will pose a fire hazard.

Don't permit portable electric heaters unless your building is wired with 20-amp circuits. If in doubt, call an electrician. Don't permit kerosene heaters under any circumstances.

• Fireplaces. Show the tenants how to work the damper and

tell them to leave it open for twenty-four hours after having a fire. Otherwise, there is the danger of asphyxiation. Incidentally, if you provide heat, don't allow the fireplace to be used during the cold winter months.

• Lighting. Tell your tenants not to turn off any lights in the public spaces or entrances unless you ask them to. Generally, you should have doorways and entry halls lighted until midnight. However, you should check with your local housing authority to find out if any appropriate laws apply.

GUESTS

A defined policy about guests will let your tenants know when a guest stops being a guest and should start paying rent. You will have already asked your tenants if they expect any long-term guests in the next year; then, as you go over the house rules, be specific about your guest policy. You don't want a tenant to move in and have an aunt and her three kids descending on the house and staying for three months. This doesn't mean you should never allow a tenant to have his or her long-lost Icelandic pen pal stay for three weeks; but making a tenant ask about a friend's two-week stay might possibly discourage guests who want to stay longer. Also, as with parties, some tenants might appreciate this policy—it serves as a good excuse for them if a mother-in-law wants to descend and see the sights! Guests add to the apartment's wear and tear and increase the noise in the house just by coming and going; they use water, generate rubbish and in general can be a burden for you.

First, tell your tenants that you would like to know in advance about any guests who will stay longer than two weeks. Specify that guests cannot bring their pets without your express permission.

Let your tenants know whether or not you'll permit guests to stay in the apartment if the tenant is away for an extended period. In general, it's a good idea to discourage this. For one thing, you can't be sure that guests will observe your ground rules as carefully as tenants do. If guests leave the doors unlocked, they put the entire house at risk. After all, if you'd wanted to buy a hotel you would have.

Be sure to let your tenants know where overnight guests should park.

PAINTING AND WALLPAPERING

Be sure your tenants are clear on this ground rule: that you do not allow any painting or wallpapering without your prior permission and that, further, you reserve the right to approve the color(s) or pattern(s). This rule should apply whether or not you pay for the paint/wallpaper or not.

If you promise to do any redecorating before or after a tenant moves in, be specific. Otherwise, your tenant may misinterpret your casual comments as you show the apartment. If you say, "Gee, I hadn't noticed how this wallpaper has faded," your tenant may think you're promising to replace it. Just as the used car dealer is careful not to make promises he can't keep, so should you be careful.

HEAT

If you pay for the tenants' heat, you should install locked thermostats which will provide the minimum warmth specified by local ordinances. Usually sixty-eight degrees during the day and sixty-four at night is required. Make sure your tenants understand they can't adjust the setting but that they should let you know if they are either too hot or too cold. You should also require tenants to keep all storm windows closed during the heating season unless the temperature outdoors exceeds sixty degrees. Tell your tenants you will raise their rent if they fail to comply. And do it.

If you do not provide your tenants with heat, you should expect them to keep the apartment heated. To make sure your tenants don't set the thermostat too low, you should lock the thermostat at the desired low level. For instance, if you live in the Northeast, you should lock the thermostat at fifty; if the thermostat were to be set much below that, the pipes could freeze or the paint could peel. You could also purchase a thermostat which does not have any settings below fifty.

UTILITIES

Your ground rules should specify what utilities your tenants are responsible for paying.

CLEANLINESS

While going over the ground rules, you should tell your tenants that you expect them to keep the apartment clean. At the same time, let them know if there are any special policies or if anything in the apartment deserves particular notice—for instance, if the cleaning mechanism in the self-cleaning oven doesn't work. Tell your tenants if you don't allow abrasive chemicals such as Bab-O or Comet to be used on wood surfaces, or excessive amounts of Drano in the toilet bowls (it can corrode the plumbing). Make sure they understand that only toilet paper is permitted to be flushed down the toilet.

Let your tenant know at the outset if any of your appliances need TLC: for instance, if the refrigerator is an older model that takes a good four hours to defrost, let your tenants know so they don't go after it with a knife!

MAINTENANCE

Some important maintenance issues are discussed in Chapter 1. If the monthly rent includes more than just the apartment (yard, driveway, porch, etc.), then your ground rules should define exactly what your expectations are, especially if you and the tenants are going to share the "extra."

• If your tenants use the yard, you'll want to specify who cuts the grass or rakes the leaves. You should also specify that your tenants pick up the yard after using it—you don't want plastic swimming pools, playpens or blankets left out for extended periods.

• If your tenants use the driveway, specify in your ground rules who is expected to shovel the snow.

• Regarding common hallways, tell your tenants if you expect them to sweep or vacuum the ones directly outside their apartment. Since their standards and yours might not dovetail, it is recommended that you assume this responsibility.

• If your tenants have the use of the laundry area, think about splitting the hours with them so you don't need to use the facilities at the same time. Be sure to let the tenants know if you want only a certain kind of soap used, if only cold-water wash is permitted, and if tenants are expected to share in the cleanup.

DECORATIONS

Once your tenants move in, they will be eager to decorate the apartment. Inevitably, the first thing they'll do is pick up a hammer and nails and put up pictures, mirrors, and assorted memorabilia on the walls. Let them know in advance what is permitted on the walls and how it should be hung.

• Draperies. Tell your tenants to use the existing curtain rods, which they shouldn't remove. Otherwise, if every successive tenant removes the rods and installs new ones, the window moldings will look like a well-used pincushion. However, if your tenants' curtains will not fit on the existing rods, take the time to install new ones yourself.

• Pictures, mirrors. Tell your tenants to use picture hangers rather than nails. The stick-on picture hangers aren't recommended because they are not sturdy. However, make it part of your policy that nothing weighing over fifteen pounds can be hung up without your being consulted.

• Plants. You should always be consulted before your tenants hang their plants. Otherwise your ceiling may become pockmarked from J-hooks, since tenants may choose to ignore the hangers left behind by their predecessors.

• Shelves. Any wall-mounted shelf should be installed professionally. Books weigh a considerable amount—the wall or floor has to be able to support a 150-pound load per square foot, as do the shelves' supports.

RENTED ROOMS

All of the preceding concerns should be yours if you rent out a room in your home, although you'll want to be extra careful to stress your concerns about noise and safety and security with your tenant. Because it is your home and your tenant will be—like it or not—very much underfoot and a part of it, you should formulate ground rules so that you and your tenant have as much, or as little, distance as you want. Take extra care to define where your space begins and what the tenant's privileges are vis-à-vis use of the telephone, entertaining guests, rooms that are off limits, and the like.

8

Dealing with Repairs and Improvements

Scene One: Three months after your new tenant moves in, you receive several bills instead of the rent check. One is for $325 from Yikes Plumbers, another is for $86.71 from Hot Stuff Electricians, and the third is for $181.24 from Extravaganza Decorators and Wallpapers. Instead of getting a check for the rent for $500, you have these three bills with a note from your tenant saying, "I'd appreciate your giving me a reimbursement check in the amount of $92.96 as soon as you can." You take a deep breath, pull out your checkbook, and knock on your tenant's door.

Scene Two: For the past three weeks, it seems as though you have heard the tenant's water running almost constantly. You knock on her door and she tells you that "the toilet seems to be running all the time." You wonder, "Did she think it would heal itself like a cut?" and then ask if she would kindly notify you as soon as she notices anything that needs to be fixed.

Scene Three: The day after your tenant moves in, she knocks on your door to tell you that the kitchen faucet leaks, the living room door sticks, the oven light doesn't work, and the water pressure in the shower is pitiful. You stop what you're doing and make the requested adjustments. The following day, she knocks to tell you that the carpeting in the bedroom is badly in need of shampooing and that she wishes there was *some* way she could reach the light fixture in the living room so she could change the bulb. You ask her to look into getting the carpet cleaned and haul out your stepladder. Two days later, after a hard day at work, you're greeted at the door by your new but by now familiar tenant and are asked if she'll be able to paint the bedroom soon and if she can borrow your hammer so she can put up some pictures. When she returns the hammer, she asks whether or not the bathtub drain has "always been that slow."

Can a repair and improvement policy be far behind?

Dealing with repairs and improvements is hardly something to look forward to as a landlord, but it is a necessary evil. As the above examples show, unless you formulate early on what your policies are you run the risk of being bothered by your tenant or of paying for repairs or improvements you did not authorize.

You have three options—doing the work yourself, letting the tenant do the work, and hiring someone else to do the work. You may or may not pay for the work done. There are three caveats to keep in mind before even thinking about paintbrushes or tile grout.

First, get your apartment into tip-top shape before your tenants move in. This will all but eliminate later requests, will make tenants feel as if they have moved into a nice space, and will, of course, enable you to charge top dollar for the unit (provided you are not subject to rent control). An additional tip: if you show the apartment in almost perfect condition but have, for example, the bedroom painted right before the tenant moves in, your tenant will think you are a veritable miracle worker or at least a saint.

Second (and this is covered elsewhere in the book), put any promises about repairs or improvements in writing, as part of your tenancy agreement. This makes it clear what is expected and prevents any misunderstandings about what should be done and who would pay for it. One landlord we know told us he had a tenant who angrily told him after a rocky year he was annoyed the landlord hadn't painted the *outside* of the house, hardly within the tenant's domain.

The third caveat is to tell any new tenants at the beginning of their tenancy (or when they make their first request) that you would like to hear about all complaints or requests after a specified amount of time—say, a week or ten days—unless there is a major problem. This "break-in" period has two purposes, both of them in your interest. Not only does it allow you to fix a number of things at once and prevent you from being called every day for a week for a fifteen-minute repair job, but it also gives tenants a chance to live in and with their new apartment. As one weary landlord told us, "In maintenance, it's a danger to do too much too soon for tenants because then they become compelled to ask for more. It's almost the more you do the more they ask for, until they just drive you stark raving mad and you end up spending an absolute fortune." He continued, "There's a tendency on the part of tenants when they move in to call you right away to see whether you'll be responsive to their requests. It's kind of a built-in thing: have we got an awful landlord or will he come when we call him? So they will all call you that first two weeks. Of course, when anybody moves into a house that he hasn't lived in previously, the things that the old people who moved out were comfortable with, the person who moves in is not comfortable with. The drippy faucet in the kitchen or that knocking radiator didn't bother the old tenant but drives the new tenant to call you. And they'll call the first day or even the second day. It's not a good idea to do an awful lot of maintenance on little things like that right away—even if you can."

So ask your tenants to make a list of small things that are bothersome and to wait ten days so you can fix everything at once.

REPAIR OR IMPROVEMENT?

Your first step when faced with a list of problems is to determine if it's a repair or an improvement; is it a functional or an aesthetic problem? Naturally, you should stress to your tenant the importance of notifying you right away about any major problems—lack of heat or hot water, leaks, electrical problems, and the like.

If a repair is needed, you should turn your attention to it right away. Certainly, you don't want the damage to get any worse. Also, depending on the sanitary or housing code statutes in your community, you may not have a choice about whether or not you are going to make a needed repair. For example, if the roof leaked and the tenant's ceiling fell in, you would probably have to fix it right away since that kind of mess creates a health hazard and you might be in violation of the housing codes if you do not fix it within a certain period of time. Don't blithely assume your tenants can indefinitely "wait" for you to repair their clogged bathroom sink drain, either. If the code indicates you must provide a bathroom with a functioning sink, then you must fix it, even if it seems like a small, frivolous job. This is another good reason to familiarize yourself with the specifics of the housing code.

By and large, it will be your responsibility to make repairs. And don't assume that you can avoid making repairs simply because your tenant rented the apartment knowing several things were in disrepair. It still will be your responsibility to maintain the apartment in conditions dictated by local ordinances. "Informed consent" does not apply. Bear in mind that housing codes are based on the concept of habitability.

Next, you should determine, if a repair is needed, who caused the problem. Is it the result of wear and tear (your problem) or carelessness (tenant's problem)?

Finally, you should decide how to proceed to get the work done. There are two philosophies of landlording that come into play here. One way of handling the issue of repairs and improvements is to let your tenants treat the apartment as if it's their own. Once they move in, they're responsible for any improvements or repairs with the exception of structural problems. This method allows the tenants to paint, wallpaper, or call the plumber or electrician, paying as they go. Alternatively, you may feel more comfortable with a management approach—you're in charge of any improvements or repairs and act as a general contractor as problems or requests arise. For a variety of

reasons, we favor the latter approach. If you abdicate responsibility to your tenants, your lessened responsibility in the short
run may lead to more responsibility after they move out. Always
think ahead to the next tenants and to *their* possible requests.
More important, letting your tenants do as they please may put
you at risk—they may not always get the required permits
(which may turn into an insurance problem if, say, the wiring
they replaced causes your house to catch fire, or a resale problem
if you want to sell). Also, the average tenant won't necessarily
do it right because the apartment is like a rented car. The tenant
can just pack up and leave, with the landlord left with all the
resultant headaches.

If you decide to oversee how and what gets done when, you
have three options for the work to be done: doing the work
yourself, letting your tenant do it to your specifications, or hiring
someone else to do it.

DOING THE WORK YOURSELF

If you are reasonably handy, and have large chunks of time, it
makes sense for you to consider doing a lot of the work in your
apartments yourself—especially if you are short on cash! Doing
the work yourself gives you the most control over who has access to your tenant's apartment (something many tenants will
appreciate), and over the quality of the work because you know
your own abilities.

Before you undertake repairs or improvements in any tenant's
apartment you should assess what is required. Ask yourself:

• Is it necessary? Always ask this question!
• Can you do the job as well as a specialist? If not, you may end
  up doing the job more than once or you may end up calling a
  specialist after all.
• Do you have the time to do the job?
• Have you carefully evaluated the scope of the job?
• Is it convenient for you and your tenants for you to do the
  job? You may think it will be a breeze for you to replaster your

tenants' ceiling over the next four weekends but they may be peeved by the end of the second one!

- Is doing the work yourself the cheapest from a tax point of view? Remember, your own labor is not deductible, while someone else's is. Also, remember that the total costs of repairs are deductible in the year they are incurred, while costs of improvements are considered capital expenditures and are subject to depreciation.

- Is the job a reasonably safe one? Don't undertake any task that puts you in danger, no matter how strapped you are for cash. If you fall off the scaffolding while repairing a tenant's cathedral ceiling, you may break your back and be out of work forever—and it's unlikely that your own insurance would cover this kind of accident. Painters, roofers and plasterers are all insured to take that kind of risk. Welcome them into your home with open arms.

In short, ask yourself: Can I? May I? Should I?

There are several advantages to doing repairs and improvements yourself. Your costs are limited to supplies and time, while your "sweat equity" will surely pay off in the future, either in a higher rent or in a profit when you sell. You have control over the quality of the work and over when the work will be done—no waiting to get estimates or to let the craftsmen in! Another advantage is a rather intangible one: if your tenants see you doing all the work yourself and see how *hard* you work, this may tend to limit their requests and may encourage them to "think economically."

On the negative side, when you attempt to do all the work yourself, you may complete the job but be in violation of certain building codes. Also, you may give your tenants ideas about other things to be done—and find yourself continually faced with, "Oh, Jim, while you're here, would you mind loosening/tightening/removing/attaching/helping me/moving/inspecting" whatever the item may be! In other words, if your tenants know you're "handy" they may not have an incentive either to maintain the premises—since they know you can, say, unclog the drain in a pinch—or to respect your time and limit their requests to those that are necessary. Finally, if tenants see you doing certain repairs, they may try to imitate you the next time there is a problem, which may turn out to be unsafe.

LETTING YOUR TENANT DO THE WORK

Letting your tenant take care of repairs and especially improvements might seem like a perfect solution, especially if your own unit needs TLC as well. Seemingly, it's free, easy and faster than doing it yourself. However, before you entrust your tenant with a hammer or paintbrush, you should ask yourself the following questions:

1. Is the work necessary? If not, who will pay for it? (The assumption here is that if it's necessary you will pay for it.)
2. Is your tenant capable of doing the work?
3. Is it a repair or an improvement?

Let's consider improvements first. As mentioned at the outset, letting a tenant do the work may be quite appealing to you. Perhaps you're inclined to provide the materials (paint, wallpaper, paintbrushes) but have the tenant do the time-consuming work. Tempting as it may be, you should consider that, even if tenants are capable of actually doing the work, by having them do the work you will shift the "power balance" slightly. Your tenants will always feel as if you owe them something.

For example, if six months after your tenants have wallpapered two rooms you determine it's time to increase the rent or even time to terminate the tenancy, how will they respond? Your tenants' work has, in fact, made the apartment more valuable, so in a sense they feel as if they have "allowed" you to charge more. In short, it clouds the issue of what the tenants are paying for. You are never going to be able to anticipate what might come up, so if you can take care of improvements yourself, do so.

There are exceptions, of course, especially if a tenant wants an improvement you don't think is necessary. For instance, we had a tenant once who wanted to repaint the *inside* of one of the bedroom closets. Since we hardly thought it was necessary and since she was fairly insistent, we allowed her to go ahead. Another improvement which you may want to let a tenant pay for is the installation of a washer and dryer hookup or of built-in shelves. These little "extras" can always be shouldered by the tenant.

If you do let your tenants fix up their apartment, by all means retain approval of paint or wallpaper colors, insist on receipts and reimburse the tenants accordingly. It's not a good idea to have your tenants simply deduct the cost of supplies from the monthly rent, mainly because it's our feeling the two transactions should be accounted for separately. It maintains the professional relationship better to account for apples and oranges separately. Also, reserve the right to inspect their progress. If, say, they're not using dropcloths, you can remedy that situation right away. Check in at the beginning of the job and at the end to be sure safe and proper cleanup has been done. You're not being nosy but are taking an interest in what is yours.

Letting the tenants take care of needed repairs can be a godsend if an emergency arises when you are away. For example, a broken window may need a new piece of glass or a badly leaking drain may have to be repaired right away. Likewise, you'll probably have warm feelings toward tenants who repair any damages they caused, such as spackling a dented wall or regrouting bathroom tile after infrequent cleaning.

However, major repairs should *never* be done by a tenant. Your risk that the tenant is a clumsy amateur is too great—you would risk having to do the work a second time. Also, allowing your tenants to do anything major could come back to haunt you—even good-natured tenants could turn around and accuse you of shirking your responsibility and being negligent.

In order to be prepared for an emergency, you should give your tenants your work phone number and the number where you can be reached in the event you are going to be away for an extended trip; in the latter case you should also supply your tenants with a list of emergency numbers, such as the numbers of the plumber, electrician, fuel company, and carpenter you most frequently deal with.

REPAIR AND DEDUCT

Sometimes tenants will make repairs themselves or hire some-one else to do them—and will deduct the cost from the rent each month until they feel they have been repaid. Usually this happens when tenants feel their requests for needed repairs have fallen on deaf ears. You should be aware that, in most cases, tenants can neither make repairs nor authorize someone else to do them unless they have followed strict steps, such as notifying you in writing prior to filing a complaint at the local housing court. If such a complaint is filed, usually the court orders you to make repairs within an appointed time, after which your tenant may commission such repairs if you have failed to make them.

WORK DONE IN EXCHANGE FOR RENT

If you are in the process of doing extensive renovations on your house, you may be tempted to trade your rental apartment for the services of a skilled tenant. Or perhaps your struggling cousin needs a place to live temporarily and offers to work for the rent. A problem can arise when your standards differ. One weary landlord who tried that route told us, "Her interpretation of the word 'work' is making the place look pretty, and our interpretation is doing it over from scratch . . . She spent her time saying, 'wouldn't a pretty painting look nice up there.' "

If you offer this kind of exchange, be cautious and specific. Itemize exactly what you expect will be done and limit it to cosmetic work unless your tenant is a licensed tradesperson. Put a time limit on the arrangement so that, say, at the end of six months you will charge full market value for the apartment. (Incidentally, this might be a difficult adjustment for tenants to make, after living rent-free all this time.) You should charge full rent and pay tenants for their services—consider the two will cancel each other out, but this system makes it crystal clear what's what.

Treat the person with respect. Just because a tenant is doing the work doesn't mean he or she doesn't have the same right to privacy as any other tenant. Don't go in on a daily basis to inspect unless you agree on it in advance, and certainly don't invite your friends to go on a walking tour of the tenant's apartment.

HIRING SOMEONE ELSE TO DO THE WORK

Even if you are handy, hiring tradespeople to do necessary work is by far the easiest solution to the repairs and improvement question. This route has many advantages. Chances are the work will be done quickly, and all at once. (In fact, you should insist that the tradesperson give you an estimated completion date so that your tenant isn't inconvenienced over a long period of time.) Secondly, since the tradesperson is hired (by you) for a specific task, such as painting a room or fixing a leaky drain, your tenant can't request that any other work be done at the same time. Thus, your tenant cannot say, "Oh, Jim, while you're here, would you mind . . . ?" Third, this route has no strings attached. Unlike having your tenants do the work and feel as if you owe them something for their efforts, this method is straightforward and direct. Also, since in most cases you will be the one who pays for the work, the tradespeople will have a sense of loyalty toward you, if anyone! They will want to do a good job for you so that you'll call them again. Fourth, in the event that you're hiring someone to repair damage caused by a tenant, a third-party tradesperson can objectively judge whether the damage is the result of abuse or normal wear and tear. Finally, a licensed tradesperson will do the work to the standards of the building code and will take care of getting proper permits.

There are several things you should consider before hiring someone. First, you should get an estimate of the cost of the work. Because you're paying for someone else's time, you should know what the total will be. You should also be clear with your tenant about who will pay for it. Second, face the fact that you will probably have to wait for an experienced craftsman to work you into his schedule. Thus, for all but emergency repairs, try to line someone up well in advance. If we had one dollar for every time the man at the oil company said, "I'll be right over to service the boiler," we'd be rich. Also, of course, factor in enough time to get several estimates. While this might seem obvious, it's easily overlooked. For example, we decided to have separate heating systems installed (versus paying for all the heat ourselves), but by the time the various representatives finally arrived to give us estimates, almost three weeks had lapsed. Then, the plumber who would do the job couldn't schedule the job for a month, so that the entire delay cost us two hundred and fifty dollars, the cost of an additional tank of oil.

Check the references of any tradespeople you are considering hiring. If you are new to the area, you may not know the various tradespeople. The best sources of recommendations are dependable people—not necessarily neighbors! Try your local hardware store. Incidentally, cultivate the places where you do your major business. In the business we're in, you'll find yourself, at least initially, spending a lot of time—to say nothing of money!—in your hardware store. If the owners are savvy, perhaps they'll offer you a modest discount and special services from time to time. One landlord we knew patronized a convenient but slightly more expensive hardware store near him, the advantage being that whenever he needed something in a hurry, whether it was a pane of glass or keys made, the owner bent over backward to accommodate him.

If you do hire a tradesperson, why not check out your other units to see if he could repair more than one thing while he's at it, saving yourself the inconvenience of having to hire him to come back in a month or so. Remember, plumbers and the like charge by the hour—and if the job only takes fifteen minutes, chances are, depending on local custom, you'll pay for a full hour. Thus, have some other chores lined up so that you get your money's worth.

The final caveat about hiring someone to do needed repairs in your apartment: make every attempt to be there at least when they first arrive. That will enable you to reiterate exactly what you want done and to show them where fuses, circuit breakers, etc., are. Also, encourage your tenant to be there for the entire time, if he or she so desires. The last thing you need is for your tenant to come to you later and complain about missing items, unlocked doors or windows, or broken and inadequate cleanup.

In most cases, you will bear the cost of having someone else do the work in your tenant's apartment. The exception would be in the event your tenant is desperate for an improvement you don't think is necessary. Some examples of this are wallpaper over a freshly painted wall, installation of shelves, and anything "extra" like terra-cotta tiles over a floor in good condition. However, tread carefully here—if your tenants pay, they will feel as if you owe them something when time comes to raise the rent.

If the work is being done as the result of a tenant's abuse or negligence, the tenant should pay for the repair. You should pay the tradesperson and bill the tenant rather than having the tenant pay the tradesperson directly. This will ensure that your valuable tradespeople are paid promptly. When you bill your tenants, be sure to give them copies of the original bills. Although you are not obligated to do so, a copy of the actual bill will show your tenant the actual cost to you. A sample bill to a tenant is shown below.

INVOICE FOR DAMAGE

January 16, 1985

To: Jim and Carol Tenant
Re: Clogged drain due to kitty litter

Yikes Plumbing (see attached bill)	$182.16
ABC Hardware (see attached receipts)	32.96
Total	$215.12

Be sure your bill includes a reference to the job itself, e.g., "Damage to hardwood floors by dog," or "Repair gouge in living room wall." If the amount your tenant owes you is substantial you could work out a flexible payment schedule, although in most cases it's advisable to have your tenant reimburse you within thirty days. Even if you have a security deposit (and if you have followed our advice, you will have one), you should not deduct from it for damage that occurs during the tenancy; better to take care of any such damage as it happens and reserve the deposit until the end of the tenancy. If it reasonably appears that the damage was not accidental but was intentional and malicious, contact the tenant immediately. Clearly, if you see your tenant tearing off the banisters or kicking your doors, don't waste a minute!

REPAIRS IN RENTED ROOMS

The issue of dealing with repairs and improvements is not as much of an issue when you rent out a room in your home. Your roomers/tenants are usually not as concerned about trying to make the space "their own." Also, since usually only a bedroom is rented, the room itself is less prone to the usual roster of repairs—leaks or malfunctions.

If your tenants do want to make cosmetic improvements, weigh the requests carefully since their taste may not dovetail with yours and since they are more likely to be transient than other tenants. Remember that it's best to allow—and pay for—neutral tones only.

Naturally, if something malfunctions in the rented room—let's say the radiator puts out only inadequate heat—then you should arrange to have it fixed. Likewise, if something that is part of your rental agreement (such as the laundry facilities) malfunctions, it is your responsibility to fix it (presuming it is shared by the rest of the house—otherwise, your tenant could pay for the repair).

Repairs or improvements to the "public space" (what there is of it) should also be your responsibility but may be handled somewhat more casually; that is, your tenant may want to pitch in and help but shouldn't feel obligated. Finally, even if your tenant offers, you should take care of repairs or improvements to your private quarters yourself. Keep business matters professional, personal matters personal.

HOW TO RESPOND TO REQUESTS

Especially if you're not someone who thinks quickly on your feet, you should plan in advance how you will handle requests for improvements or repairs. Naturally, if your tenants call and say the toilet is overflowing, don't tell them you'll think about it and call them in a week. In most cases, though, you should give yourself the time to make your own decision, except in emergency situations. Being a landlord is, first and foremost, a business. Tenants' requests almost always will require some capital outlay (of your capital); thus, you should treat such requests in a businesslike way. Regardless of the fact that your expenses may be tax-deductible (see Chapter 9), they are nonetheless capital expenses out of your pocket. As one landlord who had purchased a new stove put it—"Yeah, it's deductible but amortizing a four-hundred-dollar item over twenty years doesn't make anyone rich." If you were a farmer, you wouldn't spontaneously decide to buy new pieces of machinery; if you sold video games, you wouldn't suddenly add a line of calculators without careful thought. Approach your apartment the same way; formulate a "master plan" of improvements and maintenance that you would like to see over the next year, over the next three years, and so on. You have to act a bit more promptly with repairs, but you still should weigh each request carefully. In short, avoid making snap, costly decisions that will "nickel and dime you to death."

How then should you respond when your tenant knocks on your door? First of all, unless your tenant is coming to you with a repeated complaint, act as if you are hearing about it for the first time. No tenant wants to hear, "Oh, *that* noisy radiator. It drove the previous tenant crazy, too." Or (petulantly), "I *told* you we weren't going to repaint the living room."

The rule of thumb here is to be direct but never to make a decision on the spot. Even if you know right away that you won't go along with a request, tell your tenants you'll consider it and will let them know by the end of a week's time. Then be sure to let them know.

If the request is repair-related, you should always inspect the problem immediately. Don't take your tenant's word for it; assess the problem yourself. Even if it's obvious that you will have to have something done immediately, try to avoid making a commitment on the spot; you may not be able to honor it if you are unable to get tradespeople right away. We favor an approach along the lines of "Sounds like a job for Yikes Electricians," or else repeating the obvious: "This radiator isn't letting off any heat. Let me see what I can do."

If the request is improvement-related, chances are your tenant has thought about asking for the improvement for a while and may even have samples to show you. In rare cases, the tenant will have already purchased the supplies and is merely asking for a reimbursement. Whatever the case, don't make a commitment on the spot. Don't *ever* reimburse any tenant for expenses not previously authorized by you.

After you've heard your tenant's request and examined the situation yourself, go back to your unit and brood a bit. Remember—you have three options: (1) "Yes," (2) "No," and (3) "Let me think about it for a while." Stress that it may take you a bit of time, that your lack of an answer does not imply an affirmative answer. Always insist, in the case of paint or wallpaper, on having "veto power" and ask for samples (that is, unless you permit only certain colors to be used). One landlord we know used to let the tenant pick the color until "a couple of people decided they liked red, one person decided they liked the ceiling very dark blue. That cured us of that attitude—now we allow white." Invoke Henry Ford, who told customers, "You can have any color you want as long as it's black."

Ask yourself if allowing your tenants to have their way would in any way set a precedent. If you assent to designer wallpaper in the dining room, you may have to go along with designer wallpaper in the other rooms as well—and if your other tenants get wind of it, you may be "forced" into putting designer wallpaper everywhere! Also, keep in mind that, over the long term, you have to live with the consequences. Lovely textured wallpaper may suit your tenant's taste but may be utterly impractical. In other words, always think ahead to who your next tenant will be. On the other hand, as one landlord put it, "Let the tenants

live with their own tastes. You can assume the next person is
going to want to repaint anyway."

YOUR OBLIGATIONS

First, a word about privacy. Privacy is something most tenants, even the most reasonable, brood about. No matter how
frequently they interrupt *your* life, they don't like it when you
interrupt theirs. Repairs and improvements should, thus, be handled promptly and with respect.

Get your apartments in tip-top shape *before* renting them.
Strangely enough, a tenant would rather have a dumpy but adequate place to call home right from the start than have a chic
ultramodern apartment if it means that the apartment is a con-
struction site. Especially if you are a new landlord and are desperate to rent out your apartment so that "cash flow" will be a
real thing, it may be tempting to have your tenants move in
while the work is still going on. What's a little sawdust, plaster
or paint fumes, you might ask. Don't do it! It will get things off
to a bad start; your tenants will resent that the space is not really
"theirs"; they will rightly feel their privacy is being invaded. It
doesn't matter how good your intentions are or that, ultimately,
they'll have a wonderful space.

You may not have the right to make improvements without
your tenants' permission. Many states give the landlord the right
to enter a unit to make repairs but not to make improvements.
After all, your tenants rented the apartment "as is" (unless
promises are in writing), which indicates they were happy with it
when the lease was entered into.

Naturally, of course, if your long-term tenants ask to have
their apartment painted, then they will have no choice but to be
slightly inconvenienced.

Second, keep in mind what it is you're renting: livable space.
If your tenants cannot live in the space while work is being done,
you must see that other arrangements are made for them. If the
apartment lacks the basics—light, heat, water—then it is your
responsibility to offer other arrangements. Especially when

you're spending substantial sums on an unexpected repair, you will hate the thought of spending more money on putting your tenant up *anywhere,* but you have no choice since the space you are providing is temporarily unavailable. We don't recommend you invite your tenants to stay with you, for your and their privacy; also, if the work takes longer than expected, you'll get on each other's nerves.

Because repairs and improvements are so disruptive, your tenants may prefer that you take care of them when they are away for an extended period, which is fine if it's clear to them exactly what will be done in their absence. In any case, be sure to give the tenants plenty of notice. Sometimes even the best intentions of doing repairs or improvements on a timely basis will be interpreted as an invasion of privacy by your tenant.

REGULAR MAINTENANCE

Since you can't count on your tenant to tell you that something is going wrong with some aspect of the apartment, you really should institute a program of regular inspection so that routine things can be fixed before they become a real problem. One landlord came to this approach the hard way: "After four years I went in to clean up and found out that five light fixtures were broken and not working. There also was a plumbing problem—the toilet had been running for four months and we had a five-hundred-dollar water bill as a result."

Schedule the inspection far enough in advance to give your tenant plenty of notice. Check the drains, the toilets, doorbells, carpet and floors, ceilings, tile grout and the like.

We suggest you make inspections at the beginning, middle and end of the winter, at least, to check for leaks or other consequences of cold weather.

If you have to move the tenant's furnishings to get to, for example, the faulty outlet, ask your tenant's permission—e.g., "Jim, is it all right to move this Ming vase so I can get to the outlet? Why don't you move it—I'd hate to break it."

If you do spot a problem, mention it and set up a date to fix it. Don't race around or be accusatory if you can help it. Be conversational and let your tenant know what you think should be done.

9

The Financial Part of Being a Landlord

Chances are, if you just bought your house and are in the process of getting moved in, the last thing you have time to do is set up an accounting and record-keeping system for your apartments. You figure you can worry about it later, once you get settled. In the meantime, you use the time-honored, popular accounting method of putting everything vaguely financial in the bottom drawer of your desk. Come April 15, you reckon you can sort through it all—or have your accountant sort through it. However, you find yourself spending all sorts of unplanned-for time rummaging in that bottom drawer. First, one of your tenants asks for a second copy of the rental agreement. You can't locate it in the bottom drawer and finally find it in your safe deposit box. You don't remember why you put it there. Then, Yikes Plumbers sends you a dunning notice, when you are sure you paid the bill. If only you could find the canceled check in the drawer! Finally, you locate a veritable sheaf of canceled checks, five of which are to Yikes—but you can't find the one for the amount in question. Then, the straw that breaks this accounting system's back comes in the form of an innocent question from a fellow landlord, who asks "What's your net monthly income from your two apartments?" You realize you don't have any idea.

If this sounds familiar, then it's time to set up a bookkeeping and record-keeping system. The system you set up need not be complicated. In fact, it's inadvisable to set up a system that is wonderful but is so time-consuming and detailed that you don't use it and wind up retreating to your bottom drawer. The system you devise should be relatively easy to use once it is set up, should allow you to retrieve information without any difficulty, and should enable you to assess your cash flow and review your expenses and income on an annual basis. Ideally, from it you should be able to determine how much you spent for a specific type of expense in a given month, and in a given year. Although it may take some time to develop and fine-tune your system, once it is established it should make your life easier. Naturally, the system is only as good as the information you supply—thus, you will have to be a faithful bookkeeper. Remember as you set up a system, your goals will be facile retrieval of information and assessment of your finances.

As this chapter will show, rental housing presents a myriad of complex tax and accounting problems which are best sorted through with the help of a real estate lawyer or an accountant who has a firm grounding in the tax issues of rental housing and is up-to-date on recent changes in the law. Although it is certainly possible to "do it yourself," you should not regard this book as a substitute for professional expertise, which is highly recommended.

Should you buy a personal computer and program it with your accounting system? Probably not, unless you have more than four apartments, can justify the capital expense, or could use it in your "other" business. With a personal computer, you still would have to take the time to enter the expense data faithfully; the speed would be in the calculation. You may have so many other items calling out for your money that a personal computer may not seem like the necessity that a new furnace, roof, kitchen or bathroom is. Our suggestion is to find an accountant with a computer—someone who is willing to run through your numbers on a regular basis and at income tax time, thus providing you with the service you need. Alternatively, you might consider renting a personal computer until you assess its usefulness.

ESTABLISHING A HOUSE-RELATED CHECKING ACCOUNT

Your first step in setting up a record-keeping system is to separate your house expenses from your business expenses. Not only will this give you greater control over your cash flow; it will also make your life (and your accountant's) much simpler at tax time. Open a separate checking account that you use exclusively for your house and apartment expenses, including supplies, insurance premiums, maintenance, repairs and mortgage expenses. If you wish, you could pay into this account the amount you set aside each month as the building fund (see Chapter 2), or you could transfer money from a higher-interest account into your house checking account as needed. Always have enough in it for basic expenses, such as trips to the hardware store, emergency visits by the plumber, and the like.

If possible, open an account with overdraft privileges or a "line of credit." That way, if one of the rent checks bounces, any checks you have written will be covered. Likewise, you will have funds available in case of emergency.

With a separate checking account it will be much easier to see where your money goes, instead of having checks and expenses buried in your personal account among checks to the grocery store, hairdresser, or dry cleaner. Also, it saves you from confusing your personal and apartment expenses. For example, if you have the plumber come to your own apartment you should pay it out of your personal account, but if he comes to your tenant's apartment you should pay it out of your house account (and perhaps bill your tenant, as discussed in Chapter 8).

A separate checkbook will enable you to have a sense of whether you can afford certain repairs or supplies at a particular time. Let's say you have six hundred dollars in your house account and want to put up three new storm windows at one hundred dollars apiece, which would leave you with three hundred dollars. However, you also realize that you must pay the insurance next week, pay the utilities this week, and buy lawn fertilizer before the end of the month. These latter expenses total more than your three-hundred-dollar balance; thus, you decide to hold off a month on the storm windows. You are able to control the cash flow by planning and by assessing what you have on hand.

Every time you write a check out of your house account, enter the name of the payee, the amount, and a brief description of what was required. Over the course of a year, you may forget why you went to Central Hardware that day. If you specify right in your checkbook register what the expense was for, you will have a record and a good cross-reference for tax time. (The following example shows this.) Also, make a note on the receipt itself, indicating what it was for, and put the receipt in the "Receipts and Expenses" folder, which is explained below.

Likewise, you should record and itemize any income as deposits in the checkbook register. Deposits could include rent (and specify which tenant if you have more than one), income from coin-operated laundry facilities, interest income, tax refunds and the like. The last month's rent is considered income in the year you receive it. However, a security deposit should never be treated as income.

If you find that your expenses are seasonal, you may wish to keep a nominal amount of money in your house checking account and set up a money market account, at a higher interest rate, for the home. If you already have a personal money market account, don't mix your rental income with it; open a separate one.

Checkbook Register

CHECK NO.	DATE	CHECK ISSUED TO	AMOUNT OF CHECK		T/	DATE OF DEP.	AMOUNT OF DEPOSIT	BALANCE	
						BALANCE BROUGHT FORWARD →		500	0
101	1/5	TO/FOR Yikes Plumbers, Apt. 1 drains	233	79				−233 266	BAL 2
102	1/16	TO/FOR Smalltown Electric, Public lightng	34	00				−34 232	BAL 2
	2/1	TO/FOR Deposit, Rent, Apt. 1					852	+852 1084	BAL 2
	2/2	TO/FOR Deposit, Rent, Apt. 2					852	+852 1,936	BAL 2
103	2/15	TO/FOR Bank of Smalltown, Mortgage + taxes	1,300	00				−1,300 636	BAL 2
104	2/28	TO/FOR Village Hardware, New faucet, Apt. 1	22	91				−22 613	BAL 9 3
105	3/1	TO/FOR Smalltown Chronicle, Ad for #1 vacancy	26	90				−26 586	BAL 0 4
106	3/1	TO/FOR Lucky Insurance, casualty	389	00				−389 197	BAL 0 4
107	3/1	TO/FOR Lucky Insurance, liability	68					−68 129	BAL 4
		TO/FOR							BAL
		TO/FOR							BAL
		TO/FOR							BAL
		TO/FOR							BAL
		TO/FOR							BAL
		TO/FOR							BAL

ESTABLISHING A FILING SYSTEM

Set up manila folders for each apartment and for rejected applicants. Keep rejected applications for two years. Each apartment should have two folders: one for the applicant, filed under the person's name, and the other under the apartment address and number.

The tenant's folder would include his or her application, any notes you made to yourself when checking references, a copy of the tenant's credit report if you requested one, a copy of the rental agreement, a copy of the Apartment Condition Report, copies of receipts for first month's rent, last month's rent and the security deposit, the bank account in which the security deposit is held, copies of rent receipts if your tenant requests them (otherwise, just use the canceled check), and copies of any correspondence during the tenancy.

The apartment folder of receipts and expenses is vital to your financial operation. It will be useful when you sell your house and may be useful when you review your insurance coverage. Include in it all receipts related to the apartment, most of which will have been entered in your checkbook register. Arrange them in chronological order. Don't forget about out-of-pocket expenses or credit card receipts for purchases for the apartment. (We don't recommend you use your personal credit card for apartment expenses, but sometimes it's unavoidable.) If you pay for services or labor or supplies in cash and don't get a receipt, remember to make a note on a slip of paper and put it in the file. Label each receipt, noting what it was for. Thus, your folder could contain receipts for plumbers, supplies, reimbursement to your tenant for supplies, appliances, floors, paint, wallpaper and the like.

Why not have one folder for the apartment instead of two, one for the tenant and one for the receipts? First, having a yearly receipts folder will make your life simpler at tax time. Second, most tenants don't move in on January first—but your annual expenses for the apartment go from January to December. Third, you might have as many as four tenants in the course of a year, but the agreements and accompanying paperwork for four tenants don't have too much bearing on your financial assessment, which is computed on a January-to-December basis. Thus, for 1985, you might have tenant folders for Caroline E. Tenant, Daniel Tenant, Chris Tenant and Kit Tenant, but one expense folder, "1985 Expenses and Receipts, Apartment 1, 186 Pacific St." Once a tenant has moved, you certainly don't need the related paperwork cluttering up your finances. Also, ideally, once your tenant has moved in and has signed on the dotted line, chances are his or her folder will lie relatively dormant, while your expense folder will be added to somewhat more regularly.

You will need one more folder for house—versus apartment—expenses. As will be explained in more detail below, you will be entitled to deduct or depreciate certain expenses for the house itself. These include, for example, painting the exterior, landscaping, putting in a driveway or repairing the gutters. Thus, you will need a folder for "Receipts and Expenses, 186 Pacific St., House Matters." (Whether or not you set up a folder for your own apartment is up to you—it's recommended.)

These folders and a separate checking account form the basis for a sound record-keeping system. For many small landlords, this system is sufficient, for it easily allows one to retrieve any information. Its drawback is that it does not categorize your expenses and thereby prevents you from developing a long-term plan for your house.

INSURANCE

As part of the process of setting up a record-keeping and bookkeeping system, you should evaluate your insurance needs and coverage. Chances are, if you have a mortgage on your house, the bank or mortgage lender requires you to have a homeowner's policy which covers you in the event of fire and other casualties. Although your personal property is covered under this policy, your tenant's property is not.

Several types of additional coverage are recommended. If you have tools or special equipment valued above the "personal property" allowance, get a separate rider which covers them.

Be sure your policy covers living expenses for you and your tenants in case alternate housing is needed. Thus, if a kitchen fire renders your tenant's apartment uninhabitable for several weeks, then your insurance policy would pay for reasonable living expenses. Also, see that your policy covers "Fair Rental Value"— that is, your policy would pay the rent while the apartment is being repaired.

Invest in a liability policy over and above what your house policy provides. Many house policies provide coverage for bodily injury only up to $100,000, which is a relatively small sum in our increasingly litigious society. Often this type of liability policy is referred to as an "umbrella policy," and can cover personal injury including bodily injury, sickness, disease, death, disability, shock, mental anguish and mental injury. The cost of an umbrella policy is quite reasonable, considering what is being covered. For example, a million-dollar umbrella liability policy can cost as little as one hundred dollars per year. This kind of policy protects you if, for example, somebody falls off your porch and it's shown that you knew or should have known that the railing wasn't safe and the person ends up disabled or unable to work.

Some liability policies also provide coverage if you are sued by your tenant for wrongful eviction, wrongful entering, harassment, malicious prosecution, invasion of privacy, humiliation, libel, slander, defamation of character and other "emotional" injuries. While these may be more difficult for a tenant to prove, the cost of litigation can run into thousands of dollars, which your insurance policy would pay.

Incidentally, don't be surprised if your house insurance policy and liability policy are not from the same insurance company. For some reason, not all the big insurance companies offer additional liability coverage. In any event, the umbrella liability policy does not and should not replace your homeowner's policy.

Be sure when you request any of the above policies that your insurance agent knows how many apartments your house has, since coverage may differ depending on whether your house is, for instance, a two-family or a six-family house.

ESTABLISHING AN ANNUAL ACCOUNTING
SPREADSHEET

Perhaps you have the feeling your money isn't being spent in the right places; or you were reprimanded by your accountant for being laissez-faire, are curious about your annual expenses, or are trying to determine if you could afford to buy another piece of rental property since the one you own is so much fun; or perhaps you're feeling caught up with your apartment business —so much so, you wonder if you could learn anything from what's in the folders. If any of these apply to you, then you could definitely benefit from having a spreadsheet which will show your expenditures by month, by year and by category.

There are many ways you could categorize your expenses. From a tax point of view the simplest way is to follow the categories already established by the IRS for use on Schedule E, Supplemental Income Schedule, which you'll have to use in preparing your income tax (this is explained in more detail later in this chapter). The spreadsheet will be a third place in which you will record your expenses (the first two being the checkbook register and the Expenses and Receipts folder). It makes sense to work with the IRS categories for a while until you find you would like to break down several of the categories even further. The basic categories are as follows:

• Advertising. This would include the cost of all paid advertising for vacancies or for work to be done.

• Auto and travel. You should note the cost of mileage, tolls and gas, in addition to charges for leased cars, bus or plane trips, as they apply to your apartment. If you are very well organized, record the mileage as you go; otherwise, you can rely on your receipts to remind you where you went.

• Cleaning and maintenance. Includes janitorial service and the cost of regular maintenance on your apartment and house.

• Commissions. Includes a rental agent's fee for finding a tenant or even for collecting the rent.

• Insurance. Includes your house policy, a liability policy and car insurance.

• Interest. Includes interest on the mortgage in addition to interest paid on installment loans (as they relate to the apartment).

• Legal and other professional fees. Includes your payments to lawyers for drawing up rental agreements, assisting in evictions, writing letters to tenants on your behalf, consulting on tenant matters; and professional dues for membership in housing associations.

• Repairs. Includes any repairs you make to keep your property in good operating condition, such as repairing your house or the apartments themselves, fixing gutters, fixing floors, mending leaks, plastering, replacing broken windows. Note: improvements are not included here as an expense. Also, if your tenant pays for a repair, you may not consider it your expense.

• Supplies. Includes cleaning supplies, carpentry supplies, office supplies.

• Taxes. Includes your real estate taxes for the year in addition to any sales taxes for appliances.

• Utilities. Includes utility charges for heat, light, gas, water and sewer hookup, for the apartment or for public spaces, (e.g., lights in a public hallway).

• Wages and salaries. Includes any regular wages you pay an employee, such as a groundskeeper, snow shoveler, cleaner or janitor. Dependents can be included here. Note that your own labor cannot be counted as an expense.

• Other. This could include, for example, Publications/Subscriptions, Entertainment.

Some of the above expenses would not be fully deductible but would be prorated according to the relationship between personal and rental space.

WHAT ABOUT IMPROVEMENTS?

Improvements should be included on your annual spreadsheet, although they will not be treated in the same way on your income tax forms as the preceding expenses. The IRS defines an improvement as follows: "An improvement adds to the value of your property, prolongs its useful life or adapts it to new uses.

Putting a recreation room in your unfinished basement, panelling a den, adding another bathroom or bedroom, putting decorative grillwork on a balcony, putting up a fence, putting in new plumbing or wiring, putting in new cabinets, putting on a new roof, or paving your driveway." Further, if you make repairs or commission an architect as part of an extensive remodeling or restoration of your house, the whole job is considered an improvement.

The basic difference between repairs and improvements is that an improvement adds to the value of the property while a repair keeps your house in good operating condition. Repairs, according to the IRS, do not add to the value of your property or substantially prolong its life. However, delaying repairs instead of following a preventive maintenance schedule will drastically shorten the life of your property and healthy investment. In the long run it is more costly to defer repairs than to do preventive maintenance. In fact, if you don't paint the house, fix the leaks or repair the broken windows, chances are a buyer would pay less for it. Also, we have found that the second most important criterion held by tenants, after good location, is the overall appearance and condition of the property, inside and outside. Keeping up the condition and appearance of a property makes sound business and public relations sense.

Improvements are not claimed as a deduction in full in the year they are made; rather, they are depreciated over the life of the building or item. Repairs, on the other hand, are deducted in full in the year they occur.

You should also include tools and appliances on your spreadsheet. These would not be deducted in full on your income tax; rather, they are considered to have a "useful life" and thus are depreciated over a certain length of time. Although they may not seem like an improvement in the same way that a new deck does, they are related to improving the house in general.

HOW DOES THE SPREADSHEET WORK?

Let's look at an example of how the spreadsheet works. Across the top, you would have a column for each month. On the left-hand side, you would set up your expenses by category, as discussed above. If you read across the spreadsheet, you can add the amounts for each month and arrive at annual totals for

ddress: 186 Pacific St.
ear: 1986

Annual Accounting Spreadsheet
(in dollars)

	Jan.	Feb.	Mar.	Apr.	May	June	Totals (annual)
dvertising			27				27
uto/Travel							
leaning							
aintenance							
ommissions				405			405
surance		389					389
terest	1,000	1,000	1,000	1,000	1,000	1,000	12,000
egal & Prof. Fees							300
epairs	234	23		500			1,757
upplies				40	60	25	125
axes	300	300	300	300	300	300	3,600
tilities	34		34		34		102
ages and Salaries							
liscellaneous				25			25
(Subscription to *Landlord News*)							
nprovements					1,000 roof		1,000
ools/Appliances	700 stove	800 washer, dryer	600 refrig.	450 d-w			2,550
OTALS	2,268	2,123	2,350	2,720	2,394	1,325	22,280

each category. If you add the expenses vertically, you arrive at monthly totals. As the example shows, Carol Landlord had the highest expenses in April, which resulted in her keeping expenses to a minimum in May and June.

Ideally, you would have one spreadsheet for each apartment and one for the house itself, with all figures (mortgage, interest, etc.) prorated accordingly. Practically speaking, however, this is a substantial amount of paperwork, so it's best to start with one spreadsheet for the entire operation. Then, if you wanted to look at the expenses for your individual apartments, you would pull each apartment's expense folder and figure from there.

HOW DOES DEPRECIATION WORK?

Depreciation assumes that all property has a finite life. Under the latest IRS rulings, real property placed in service after March 15, 1984, is assigned a life-span of eighteen years. Depreciation assumes that property or equipment related to any business has a useful life and that you should be compensated for its wearing out. Depreciation assumes that your house is worth less, in a real sense, as the years go by because it is wearing out. Depreciation applies only to rental housing; that is, personal residences may not be depreciated. Thus, if you own your house and rent out part of it, you may only depreciate that portion which is rented. Also, depreciation is based only on the house itself, not on the house and the land it is on, the theory being that land never wears out.

The marvelous thing about depreciation is that it is not a tangible expense. In fact, while you claim depreciation deductions, your property is probably increasing in value. Also, of course, chances are your house will last more than eighteen years; perhaps it's over a hundred years old now. But, on the other hand, the systems within it wear out and may be subjected to more wear and tear than if only you lived in the house.

For property that you bought after 1980, you must figure your depreciation deductions under the accelerated cost recovery system (ACRS). However, if you owned your property before 1981, you must continue to use the same method of figuring depreciation that you used in the past. You may use an alternate method of figuring your deductions, based on the straight-line method of depreciation, in place of the ACRS method. If you choose the alternate method, you may take deductions over a longer period of time. For real property, you could choose to depreciate over fifteen, thirty-five or forty-five years.

You may depreciate other property, as well as your house, over three-year, five-year or ten-year periods. You most likely own five-year property; this would include appliances, tools and equipment, and so on.

Your decision on the method of depreciation will have serious consequences when you decide to sell your house, which is all the more reason to seek a professional's advice in setting your long-range goals. For a thorough review of depreciation, see IRS Publication #534, "Depreciation."

HOW DO YOU FIGURE YOUR DEPRECIATION DEDUCTION?

Under the ACRS method, the deduction is figured by multiplying your "basis" by a percentage, as specified in the tables in the IRS booklets "Depreciation" and "Rental Property." The percentage varies from year to year and depends on when you "placed the property in service" and on the type of property (house vs. equipment).

Under the straight-line method, you would divide your basis by the number of years in the recovery period and would deduct the same amount every year. Two other methods are the declining balance method and the sum of the years' digits method.

WHAT IS THE "BASIS"?

Simply, the basis is usually the cost or value of the rental portion of the property minus the worth of the land, which often can be figured by your real estate taxes.

For example, you paid $100,000 for your four-family house, in which you live. The property tax was based on assessed values of $10,000 for the land and $90,000 for the house. Your basis would thus be $67,500 ($90,000 × 75%).

The "adjusted basis" is the basis plus the sum of any improvements.

WHAT IF ONLY PART OF THE PROPERTY IS RENTED?

If your house has three apartments in addition to your own, for example, they should be treated as though they were separate pieces of property from your personal apartment.

Some of your expenses may be deducted in full if they pertain directly to the rented portion of the property. Let's say you paint a room in a tenant's apartment, pay premiums for a liability insurance policy for the apartment, place several newspaper ads to find a tenant, pay your attorney to review your lease agreement, and pay the plumber to unclog the tenant's kitchen sink. All of these would be fully deductible on your income tax.

Other expenses may also be deducted, but only in part. Expenses that apply to the entire running of the house would have to be prorated according to your apartment's proportional relation to the rented apartments. For instance, if you have the exterior of the house painted, you cannot deduct the full amount; rather, you would be able to deduct that portion which reflects the rental portion in relation to your living space. Using the above example, you would be able to deduct three quarters of the painting expense.

Depreciation is treated in the same way as expenses. If you make improvements to your tenant's apartment—anything from providing new appliances to building a deck—you may depreciate them in full. Thus, a four-hundred-dollar stove with a life of five years could be depreciated at the rate of eighty dollars per year.

Likewise, if you make improvements to the house as a whole

or to the exterior, you would depreciate accordingly, in proportion.

How do you figure the proportions for expenses and depreciation? Common sense dictates here. Basically, you have two options: by number of rooms in the house or by area. For example, if your house consists of four apartments of equal size, one of these being your own, you would be able to deduct 75 percent of any common expenses. If your heating bill for the year for the entire house was $2,000, you would deduct $1,500 ($2,000 × 75%) as a rental expense. The balance, $500, would be your personal expense, and would not be deductible. You would follow the same system if the rental apartments and your personal apartment are not of equal size. For example, if your personal five-room apartment is part of a fifteen-room house, you would be able to deduct 66 percent of any expenses that must be divided (10 rooms ÷ 15 rooms). You could also calculate the square footages and figure the proportions this way.

If you rent out a room in your home, you would also have the option of dividing expenses according to the number of people involved. This would allow for two people sharing a room, for instance.

FACING THE TAXMAN

Before tax time rolls around, you should familiarize yourself with two government publications, "Rental Property, #527" and "Depreciation, #534." They give a succinct overview of what the regulations are and tell you what forms you will need to fill out.

In addition to filling out your regular 1040 form, you will have to fill out Schedule E, Supplemental Income Schedule, which is the form used for rental income. You will primarily be concerned with Part I of the form, which is quite straightforward. You enter your total rental income—including, incidentally, any advance rents but not necessarily security deposits—from all apartments and deduct your expenses and depreciation.

The expenses are categorized as we recommend; thus, you may take your annual expenses directly off your expense spreadsheet.

If you bought your house after 1980 (or, as the IRS puts it, "put your house in service" after 1980), then you also need to fill out Form #4562, "Depreciation and Amortization," which comes with a separate page of instructions delineating type of property, life of property, etc. Otherwise, you will fill out Part V of Schedule E. In either case, discuss it with your accountant.

Both your expenses and your depreciation deduction are then subtracted from your net rental income to calculate your net profit or loss. Don't feel like a failure if you show a loss—you have entered the netherworld of real estate where losses are really gains! Don't think of this as the latest high-tech venture—if you have been prudent with your expenditures, you want your house to show a loss, at least initially.

For example, Carol Landlord owns a town house with apartments on the first two floors. She bought the house for $100,000 and charges $810 per month for each of the two apartments, following the formula given in Chapter 2. One of the apartments had a change in tenants in late winter, so that by the end of the year Carol had collected ten months' rent for that apartment plus the last month's rent, for eleven months' total. The other apartment's tenant moved in on the first of February. Thus, Carol collected $17,820 in rents ($810 × 2 apartments × 11 months).

What were Carol's expenses? From her spreadsheet, she quickly could fill in Schedule E. She spent $26.90 to run a small ad to fill the apartment, which didn't pull at all. She struck a deal with a real estate agent, who found her a tenant and charged only half a month's rent, $405, for her services. She paid $389 for house insurance, which she prorated, charging two thirds of it, or $259.07, as an expense. In addition, she took out a $1 million liability policy for $68. Since the policy was specifically addressed to future possible claims of her tenants, she claimed the entire amount as an expense.

Carol's total mortgage interest payments for the year were $12,000. Two thirds, or $8,000, was claimed as an expense.

Carol paid $3,600 in real estate tax for her house; two thirds, or $2,400, was claimed.

To draw up rental agreements, Carol paid her attorney $250. In addition, Carol joined the local landlords' coalition and paid annual dues of $50.

Carol spent $204 on public utilities for lighting in the hallways and laundry areas.

Thus, Carol's expenses look like this:

Advertising	=	$26.90
Commissions	=	405.00
Insurance	=	259.07
Interest	=	8,000.00
Legal and professional fees	=	300.00
Repairs	=	1,756.70
Supplies	=	125.00
Taxes	=	2,400.00
Utilities	=	204.00
Other (insurance)	=	68.00
Total expenses	=	$13,544.67

Carol also may deduct depreciation expenses. In June she had a new fence installed at a cost of $1,000. She decided to outfit the apartments with new appliances, since the other mechanical systems were in relatively good condition. She bought two stoves at a cost of $350 each, a washer and dryer for the tenants' use at a total cost of $800, one new refrigerator at a cost of $600, and a new dishwasher at a cost of $450.

When Carol bought the house, the house was assessed at $90,000 and the land at $10,000. In the first year, she made several improvements. She had a new roof put on the house at a cost of $5,000 and new bathrooms installed in the tenants' apartments at a total cost of $6,000. These improvements are added to the basis for the "adjusted basis" on which depreciation for the life of the house is based, as follows:

Value of rental portion of house	=	$59,940
Cost of new bathrooms	=	6,000
Cost of new roof	=	5,000
Adjusted basis	=	$70,940

To figure depreciation, Carol uses the ACRS system of depreciation and an eighteen-year useful life. Her first-year depreciation is figured at 9 percent (per the IRS tables), but since she occupies one third of the house, she prorates it.

Carol figures her depreciation as follows:

Depreciation on house (70,940 × 9% × 66%)	=	$4,213
Depreciation on stoves (700 × 15%, five-year property)	=	105
Depreciation on washer & dryer (800 × 15%)	=	120
Depreciation on refrigerator (600 × 15%)	=	90
Depreciation on dishwasher (450 × 15%)	=	68
Depreciation on fence (1,000 × 8%)	=	80
Total depreciation	=	$4,676

Now, Carol may calculate her profit or loss on her house, as follows:

Total rents	$17,820
Less expenses	13,545
	4,275
Less depreciation	4,676
Loss	($401)

Carol's loss of $401 (see Schedule E, line 25) would be entered on Form 1040, line 18.

FACING A NEW YEAR

Many accountants will tell you that "real estate is the best tax shelter there is." Many tenants will feel, deep down, that you're getting rich at their expense. Who's right? While there are un-mistakable tax benefits that accompany the ownership of rental property and other businesses, it's our feeling that, without them, there would be no incentive to put one's money into rental housing. And the number of apartments would shrink. As it is, very little new rental housing is being built because, in spite of tax advantages, legislation and regulations make it difficult for builders and investors to build rental housing that is affordable.

As for tenants who may feel you are unjustly compensated, don't forget you are the one who gives up your freedom to spend your money as you please, to be devil-may-care, and to take off cross-country without telling anyone. Good landlords give up a lot of time and energy—time and energy that tenants spend go-ing away weekends, out to dinner several times a week, sitting in front of the television, or making lists of things they would like their landlords to do! You're the one who is "on call," and while you may not have a beeper to prove it, your responsibilities are many and your financial demands are heavy. You're the one who may be interrupted on Christmas day by a call from a vacation-ing tenant who asks you to check her goldfish tank, or on Thanksgiving by a tenant who has no hot water and a houseful of guests. When you go to investigate you practically feel like a stereotypical landlord who has deliberately willed his tenant's hot water off. Let's face it, being a landlord is often a thankless job in which you're the ogre. No matter what you do, you're still the landlord. If incentives weren't provided to help you keep up with maintenance, repairs and aggravation, you'd be an endan-gered species!

SCHEDULE E
(Form 1040)

Department of the Treasury
Internal Revenue Service (O)

Supplemental Income Schedule

(From rents and royalties, partnerships, estates, and trusts, etc.)

▶ Attach to Form 1040. ▶ See Instructions for Schedule E (Form 1040).

OMB No. 1545-0074

19**84**

13

Name(s) as shown on Form 1040	Your social security number
Carol Landlord	000 : 000 : 000

Part I   Rent and Royalty Income or Loss

1 Did you or a member of your family use for personal purposes any rental property listed below for more than the greater
of 14 days or 10% of the total days rented at fair rental value during the tax year? . . . . ☐ Yes ☐ No

2 **Description of Properties** (Show kind and location for each)

Property A ..... 186 Pacific St., Yourtown, USA ....

Property B ....

Property C

Rental and Royalty Income		Properties			Totals (Add columns A, B, and C)	
		A	B	C		
3 a Rents received (810 × 2 × 11 mos)		17,820			3	17,820
b Royalties received . . .						

Rental and Royalty Expenses								
4 Advertising	4	26	90					
5 Auto and travel.	5							
6 Cleaning and maintenance . .	6							
7 Commissions	7	405						
8 Insurance (213)	8	259	07					
9 Interest (213 a total) . . .	9	8,000						
10 Legal and other professional fees . .	10	300						
11 Repairs	11	1,757	00					
12 Supplies	12	125						
13 Taxes (Do **not** include Windfall Profit Tax here. See Part III, line 37.) . .	13	2400						
14 Utilities	14	204						
15 Wages and salaries	15							
16 Other (list) ▶								
..... Liability Insurance		68						
....								
....								
....								
....								
....								
....								
....								

17 Total expenses other than depreciation and depletion. Add lines 4 through 16	17	13,544	97		17	
18 Depreciation expense (see Instructions), or depletion	18	4,676			18	
19 Total. Add lines 17 and 18	19	18,220	97			
20 Income or (loss) from rental or royalty properties. Subtract line 19 from line 3a (rents) or 3b (royalties) .	20	(400	97)			

21 Add properties with profits on line 20, and write the total profits here	21	
22 Add properties with losses on line 20, and write the total (losses) here	22	( )
23 Combine amounts on lines 21 and 22, and write the net profit or (loss) here	23	(401)
24 Net farm rental profit or (loss) from Form 4835, line 49	24	
25 Total rental or royalty income or (loss). Combine amounts on lines 23 and 24, and write the total here. If Parts II, III, and IV on page 2 do not apply to you, write the amount from line 25 on Form 1040, line 18. Otherwise, include the amount in line 39 on page 2 of Schedule E	25	(401)

For Paperwork Reduction Act Notice, see Form 1040 Instructions.

Schedule E (Form 1040) 1984

Form **4562**	**Depreciation and Amortization**	OMB No 1545-0172

Department of the Treasury
Internal Revenue Service (O)

▶ See separate instructions.
▶ Attach this form to your return.

19 84
67

Name(s) as shown on return: Carol Landlord

Identifying number

Business or activity to which this form relates: 186 Pacific St, Youtown, USA (Rental House)

Part I Depreciation

For transportation equipment (e g. autos), amusement/recreation property, and computer/peripheral equipment placed in service after June 18, 1984, and used 50% or less in a trade or business, the section 179 deduction is not allowed and depreciation must be taken only on line 2(h).

Section A.—Election to expense recovery property (Section 179)

A. Class of property	B. Cost	C. Expense deduction

1 Total (not more than $5,000). (Partnerships or S corporations—see the Schedule K and Schedule K-1 Instructions of Form 1065 or 1120S) . . . .

Section B.—Depreciation of recovery property

A. Class of property	B. Date placed in service	C. Cost or other basis	D. Recovery period	E. Method of figuring depreciation	F. Deduction
2 Accelerated Cost Recovery System (ACRS) (see instructions): *For assets placed in service ONLY during taxable year beginning in 1984*					
(a) 3-year property					
(b) 5-year property		2,550	5 yr.	PRE	383
(c) 10-year property		1,000	10 yr.	PRE	80
(d) 15-year public utility property					
(e) 15-year real property— low-income housing					
(f) 15-year real property other than low-income housing					
(g) 18-year real property		70,940	15	PRE	4213
(h) Other recovery property				S/L	
				S/L	

3 ACRS deduction for assets placed in service prior to 1984 (see instructions) . . . .

Section C.—Depreciation of nonrecovery property

4 Property subject to section 168(e)(2) election (see instructions) . . . .
5 Class Life Asset Depreciation Range (CLADR) System Depreciation (see instructions) . . . . . .
6 Other depreciation (see instructions) . . . .

Section D.—Summary

7 Total (Add deductions on lines 1 through 6). Enter here and on the Depreciation line of your return (Partnerships and S corporations—DO NOT include any amounts entered on line 1.) . . . . | $4,676

Part II Amortization

A. Description of property	B. Date acquired	C. Cost or other basis	D. Code section	E. Amortization period or percentage	F. Amortization for this year

Total. Enter here and on Other Deductions or Other Expenses line of your return . . . .

See Paperwork Reduction Act Notice on page 1 of the separate instructions.

Form **4562** (1984)

U S GOVERNMENT PRINTING OFFICE 1984—423-237 (31-0598032)

10

*The Most Common
Hassles and How to
Deal with Them*

No book about being a landlord would be complete without a
chapter on the common hassles landlords encounter. Many but
not all hassles can be avoided if you are careful to rent to a
reliable tenant, screen applicants carefully, lay out your ground
rules, and clearly define what is for rent. Even if you are judi-
cious, however, you can still encounter hassles, either as the
result of something the tenant does, like bouncing a rent check
or playing loud music, or as the result of something you do, such
as raising the rent or otherwise changing the terms of the tenancy.

Many landlords experience hassles with their tenants precisely
because they do not take the time to formulate a set of ground
rules for the house. When a tenant's stereo blares loudly until all
hours of the morning, the landlord is irritated and tells the tenant to turn it down. The tenant, in turn, is irritated for being
chastised and feels justifiably miffed that the landlord didn't let
him know what the noise policy was before he moved in. He
wonders if there are other rules he is as yet unaware of, and may

even "test" the landlord's limits. A cycle of poor communication begins and is terribly hard to set right. In the area of landlord-tenant relations, an ounce of prevention is definitely worth a pound of cure.

The common hassles are in the eye of the landlord. Ninety-nine percent of the time you—not your tenant—are the one who will feel inconvenienced or affected. Unless you do something about it, you will be the one to lose out, since your tenants may be unaware they are doing something to "hassle" you.

Your first step in dealing with a hassle is to decide whether or not it is an isolated incident or is part of a pattern. That is, if your tenant has the stereo playing loudly while she is vacuuming on a Saturday afternoon, you probably won't rush to evict her. However, if she repeatedly plays her stereo loudly, despite your firm demands that she observe your house rules about noise, you may have no choice but to initiate eviction proceedings. On the other hand, you have to be sensible—it may be an isolated incident if your tenant sets your house on fire only once, but you certainly won't want to give that tenant a second chance by waiting to see if a pattern develops.

If you notice a pattern developing, you will also want to decide if the tenant is acting in a premeditated fashion or is simply forgetful. Is she playing her music loudly just to irritate you? Does she seem the type who would want to harass you? Or, is she making an error of judgment—does she forget how loud her speakers sound when she plays a certain kind of music?

Many of these hassles begin as small, isolated incidents and snowball into situations that are not remediable. To prevent this from happening, you should always correct the situation immediately and directly. Don't overlook a transgression even if it is an isolated incident—correct it to ensure it remains a one-time occurrence. However, use your good judgment and give your tenant the benefit of the doubt, while taking into account how long the tenant has lived in the house. As Doreen Bierbriar, the author of the useful book *Living with Tenants,* advises, "Before you become a landlord, keep both eyes open. Afterwards, keep one eye shut." If someone has been a good tenant for a year and plays music loudly one day, you probably won't run upstairs immediately. On the other hand, if someone has just moved in and turns on the music, then you have no choice but to remind that tenant of your house rules. In the latter situation, you want to nip loud music in the bud—if you fail to correct it your tenant may assume it doesn't bother you.

Your goal in dealing with hassles is to deal with each one only once. You certainly don't want to have to tell your tenant to turn down the volume on a regular basis any more than your tenant wants to listen to you do that. Always be firm and direct. Never ask tenants to do something differently—tell them instead. If you ask them, it will seem as if they are doing you a favor by complying. This is hardly the case. You as the landlord are entitled to insist that certain rules be followed.

It's best not to let something fester. If something your tenant does irritates you, you owe it to both of you to clear the air and to state your grievance. If you sit in your apartment brooding about something, you're going to get paranoid and think that your tenant is maliciously being insubordinate when in fact she may be merrily playing her music without realizing just how irritated you are. That's not to say that you should rule out the possibility that your tenant *is* in fact being deliberate; but you have to deal with the situation first before you can tell. Be optimistic when you first approach your tenant. Hope for the best. Be objective and listen carefully to your tenant's point of view, if she offers it.

Pay attention, however, to your tenant's reaction when you approach her. Does she seem cooperative or belligerent? Does she rush to turn down the volume or does she become argumentative? It's advisable that you not get into a verbal tussle. Simply state your objection, offer your required remedy, end the discussion there, and let your tenant know you expect it won't happen again.

The real test of your effectiveness is whether or not your tenant does it again. If, five minutes after you get settled in your apartment, you hear loud music again, you should seriously consider adjusting the relationship with your tenant—for instance, you could change the terms of the tenancy so that no music at all is allowed after certain hours—or warning the tenant that you are considering terminating the tenancy altogether.

Some hassles—the rent check bounces or never appears—demand your immediate attention. If you ignore them, you'll lose your credibility as a landlord to be reckoned with. Some situations, however, require flexibility on your part. Weigh being picky against being reasonable. If your tenants are new, try not to knock on their door every other day to tell them that something *else* is wrong, just as you hope they won't knock on yours. Give yourself time to adjust to new tenants before blowing the whistle. You may not be used to their individual life-style; adjust to that. In other words, don't create a hassle where there is none. Ask yourself if the music is really too loud or if perhaps it's not to your taste. In other words, don't be in a hurry to bring hassles on you both. On the other hand, never overlook or ignore a valid or serious problem—it's only guaranteed to get worse.

The rest of this chapter discusses some of the situations likely to breed hassles between you and your tenants and ways of dealing with them. If you never experience any of these, then you should buy another building or hire yourself out as a tenant selector. If, on the other hand, several ring true, take heart: chances are, in the course of being a landlord, you won't run into all of them!

RAISING THE RENT

A landlord supplies space and a home in return for compensation. A landlord also expects to get a fair return on his or her investment. When costs, such as utilities or taxes, increase or when a building needs a substantial repair, such as a new roof, the income from the apartments has to increase for the landlord to cover these expenses.

Few landlords relish reviewing their finances and realizing that they will have to raise the rent to continue to keep their heads above water. And, no tenant likes to have the rent go up. However, for many landlords faced with rising costs it is an inevitable course of action.

There are three schools of thought about raising the rent. The first is: don't. According to followers of this school, you should set the rent high enough so that you won't have to raise it during the entire course of the tenancy, whether it's one or ten years. This way, you encourage good tenants to stay and you don't run the risk of a good tenant leaving as the result of an increase. This school of thought is usually advocated by landlords who have fixed-rate mortgages and whose tenants pay all utilities. The only fixed cost is the mortgage which can be paid by the rent. However, maintenance costs are not fixed and will rise ahead of an unadjusted rent, resulting in a situation where the landlord is shortchanged.

The second school of thought advocates raising the rent on an irregular, ad hoc, catch-as-catch-can basis. Its disciples sit down every so often, pull out their shoeboxes of records and receipts, decide somewhat arbitrarily to raise the rent, and come up with the amount by magic.

The third school of thought advocates raising the rent on a regular, annual basis, whether or not their costs have increased or their tenants will move. Landlords who follow this school figure that "everything else is going up" and their rents might as well go up along with it.

Our recommendation is a two-part compromise: let your tenants know that their rent will be reviewed but not necessarily increased every year or at an expected interval. If your tenants know in advance their rent will be reviewed, they will not be surprised to get an increase (they may be unhappy but at least they won't be surprised!). They will be delighted if you decide against raising it, too. All the way around, this system is a good one. Naturally, you can only raise the rent if you are not subject to rent control.

If you decide an increase is necessary, your first step in increasing the rent is to send each tenant a written notice of the impending increase. Specify what the old rent was, what the new rent will be, how much the increase is, and what the effective date is. For instance:

January 1, 1986

Dear John Smith:

  Because of my ever-increasing costs, I'm sorry to
inform you that I have to increase your rent of $400
by $25 to $425 per month, effective April 1,
1986 .

Sincerely,

Mary Jones

Also, it helps to smooth the waters if you combine the increase
with an improvement to the tenant's apartment, if one is in the
cards. For instance, let's say your tenant has asked for a new
kitchen floor or a set of shelves in the bathroom. Taking care of
this kind of small improvement is a nice gesture. However, be
careful not to imply that the increase is going to finance the
improvement—your tenant may try to talk you out of making
the improvement! Most tenants would prefer to go without a
new floor than have their rent increased. Or, you might want to
make overall house improvements at the same time—have your
house painted, have a new roof or storm windows installed,
spruce up the common hallways or laundry area. One other
possibility is to give the tenant a little extra something at the
same time you increase the rent—for instance, you might give
the tenant use of the laundry facilities, storage space or parking.
One landlord we know whose tenant paid extra for the use of the
laundry raised the rent but had the new rent include the laundry.
Combining the increase with some kind of improvements makes
you seem benevolent, genuinely concerned about the tenant, and
responsible rather than a money-grubbing landlord.

  How much lead time should you give a tenant? Common wisdom suggests one month (provided, of course, you're not restricted by the terms of a lease), the rationale being that it
doesn't give tenants much time to look around for another unit
and practically guarantees that they will stay put. By contrast, if
you have good tenants, try to give them three months' notice
(don't, incidentally, review their rent in January and have the

increase effective the first of April—review it so that the increase
is effective at the appointed time of review). If you give ample
notice, you allow your tenants to make plans accordingly. If
they can afford the increase, then they can budget for it. If they
can't, they have three months to find a new spot and to give you
notice. It works out all around.

How much of an increase is fair? A general rule of thumb is
that anything over 10 percent is excessive. The converse is that if
you have to raise a tenant more than 10 percent then you haven't
been charging enough all along or you haven't increased on a
regular basis. Many a landlord wakes up one day to realize that
a 25 percent increase is in order. Even if you haven't increased
the rent in several years, this is still rather a big increase for a
tenant to absorb all at once. It's far better to schedule modest
regular increases than to impose haphazard irregular ones. Your
tenants will quickly forget that you haven't increased their rent
in five years and will focus exclusively on the high new rent—
and they'll resent it.

If you want to keep your tenants—and a good tenant is often
worth keeping, unless you want to have to prepare the apartment for a new one—then you should ask yourself if your tenants can pay the increase. You will, of course, be able to determine this if you have their application on file; you can look at
their income to see if it will support an increase. In fact, when
you screen for tenants, it's a good idea to rent to someone who
not only can afford your asking rent but also would be able to
afford an increased rent in the future. You'll be limited if you
rent to someone who can barely afford your asking rent.

If you have more than one apartment, should you increase all
your tenants at once or should you handle increases on an individual basis? On the one hand, if you apply the increase to two
tenants at once, you get it out of the way for the year (or whatever your review schedule is). However, this can be tricky: you
may create hard feelings if you review the rents at the same time
and decide on an increase for one of the tenants but not for the
other. You would, of course, have good reasons for doing so—
one tenant's rent may have been excessively low while the other
tenant may have come upon financial hard times—but you run

the risk of the first tenant being angry and resentful. You run less risk that the tenants will compare notes if you review the rents individually rather than all at once.

Should you give a reason when you raise the rent? You're less likely to encounter resistance and will seem credible if you do. A reason softens the blow—a tenant can't very well argue with, for instance, increased costs of fuel, property taxes, or a leaky roof. You'd be wise, however, to keep your reason structure-related. No tenant wants to pay more rent because your profit margin hasn't been high enough! One astute landlord used this strategy when his tenants requested a meeting after he last raised the rent. "I didn't go into great details about financing," he told us, "but I said basically that I didn't think it was an unfair rent—in fact, I thought it was still low for the neighborhood, and that the house is an investment like any other investment and I would be losing too much money if I didn't raise it at least somewhat, with what it was worth, and that was it."

What should you do if your tenant argues with the amount of the increase or wants to negotiate the amount? Should you negotiate? No, you shouldn't. The only situation in which you should be willing to negotiate is if the tenant has just lost his job or has otherwise been hit hard financially. If that's the case, then you should press the tenant for his plans—how is his search for a new job going, does he have a reserve out of which he will be able to pay the rent—and then reschedule the rent review for several months down the road. Don't be vague: "Gee, Jim, I'm sorry. Let's talk again soon." Be direct about it: "Gee, Jim, I'm sorry to hear that. I can hold your rent where it is now for the next two months but will have to have the increase effective at that time and will have to ask you to pay me the difference once you get back on your feet."

Aside from negotiating with a tenant who has lost his job, you should never enter into discussions about rent increases with your tenants. After all, setting the rent is the exclusive privilege of the landlord; tenants shouldn't think they can set the rent, which is what they are doing if they argue with you about it or try to negotiate.

When you increase the rent you are saying, "The apartment is

worth the increase." When tenants try to negotiate they are telling you, "The apartment is not worth the new rent." Clearly, if
they thought it was worth it, they wouldn't try to get it for less.
Also, if they can afford the existing rent, they can afford an
increase, provided it's not an excessive one. Perhaps they just
think they can't afford it—part of your job at this point is to
convince your tenants that they *can* afford it. After all, surely
they can give up something to meet the new rent rather than
expect you, the landlord, to give up something—i.e., the increase. Impress upon each tenant that the new rent is what you
need—versus what you want—to run the house effectively. Em-
phasize how minimal the increase is on a weekly or daily basis.
Let's say you increased the rent from $400 per month to $425
per month. Point out that a $25 increase is a mere $6.25 per
week, or $0.83 a day. This approach will make your tenants feel
petty and sheepish. Suggest that they check the advertisements
for apartments in your area and make them aware that the new
rent you are charging is either at or below market rate and offers
considerable amenities. (You should have, of course, already
done this yourself before setting and increasing the rent.) If you
have improved an apartment since the tenant moved in, mention
this, too.

If a tenant challenges either your right to increase the rent,
your reasons for the increase, or the amount of the increase,
don't back down. You have every right to set the rent (depending
on rent control statutes) and to expect fair compensation for
your tenants' use of the space. Avoid going into financial details,
if possible. If you want your tenants to know exactly how much,
for instance, your taxes went up, feel free to share this information with them but don't feel that you have to get down to the
nitty-gritty of your finances. Sometimes opening the door to that
kind of probing discussion opens the floodgates and encourages
tenants to be downright nosy. On the other hand, if your increase results from a valid unexpected expense, a simple explanation may cause the tenant to cease negotiating: "Jim, my taxes
went up two hundred and forty dollars, which is reflected in the
ten-dollar increase. It's only fair we both absorb it."

What should you do if Jim offers to do something around the

house in exchange for keeping the rent the same? Let's say he offers to shovel the walk on a regular basis, paint the common hallways, or build bookcases for the living room, for example. Tell the tenant you appreciate his interest but cannot agree to that solution. Keep money as the medium of exchange. First of all, it would be quite difficult to put a value on your tenant's work. What if you agreed to have him shovel snow and you have no snow that winter? Would you be justified in asking him to do something else? How many months' worth of rent does painting a hallway add up to? When does his "offer" expire? This solution to your rent increase really muddies the waters. Second, if you make this kind of arrangement with one tenant, then your other tenants are going to want to strike a similar deal. And who could blame them? If you do it for one tenant, you really are going to have to do it for everyone. You might end up with the cleanest sidewalks in town but you might not be able to pay your new tax bill!

Should you excessively raise the rent when you want a tenant to give notice—in other words, use the increase as a method to get a tenant out? Some landlords swear that this can work effectively and can prevent them from having to give notice to their tenants, since it puts the onus for leaving on the tenant. While it may work in some cases, it also might backfire. Some tenants might overly protest the increase but finally agree to it, which would still leave you stuck with them (albeit a bit richer!).

What about raising the rent for preexisting tenants? Let's say you just bought the house and the apartment on the first floor is vacant, but the one on the second floor has a woman who pays $400 a month. You know that if it were empty you could charge $475 without a hitch. Should you raise her rent accordingly? If you don't care whether or not she moves, go ahead. However, if you would like her to stay, try to keep her rent as low as you can. It's probably a good idea to increase her rent nominally to establish yourself quickly as the new landlord.

FAILURE TO PAY THE RENT ON TIME

On the second of every month, thousands of landlords are drumming their fingers on their kitchen tables, wondering where the rent checks are. By the fifth of the month, this same group of landlords is beginning to get downright frantic. Most landlords, especially those who operate on a small scale, have a limited cash flow and count on the monthly rent to pay their mortgages and taxes. When the rent is late, it can have severe consequences on the monthly budget.

Some landlords are more casual than others when it comes to tenants who pay late. They are calm as the second, third and fourth of the month roll by, and they blithely accept checks on a day later than the appointed one. Accepting the rent late without sternly telling the tenant that the rent is due on the first is comparable to letting your employer pay you when he or she feels like it. Conversely, tenants who don't pay their rent on time are taking advantage of you and may indeed take other liberties in the future.

It's irritating when a tenant doesn't pay on time. You as the landlord provide the apartment in exchange for the rent. When the rent is late, you are in a sense providing credit—your tenant has the full use of the space, but you don't have the rent.

You should, of course, at the outset, let your tenants know when you expect the rent and that you will consider it a grievous offense if it is late. Explain that your mortgage and other house-related expenses are due on the first and that you must insist that the rent be paid on the first. Incidentally, most courts will back you up on this; you have the right to receive the rent when it is due.

Even if your tenants have always religiously paid on the first, don't give them the benefit of the doubt or assume the rent will be forthcoming. Ask where it is. You could knock on the door and say, "Carol, I was just going over my books and noticed that your rent is past due, so I thought I would come by and collect it." You'll then find out if Carol has a legitimate excuse or not. If her excuse is legitimate, you will in any case want to encourage her to come forward earlier if a similar situation were to arise again.

The rent might be late merely because Carol is flaky! If, when you approach her, she tells you she had no idea it was the second of the month, you might want to change your method of rent collection to compensate for this peculiarity in your tenant. If you don't already do so, tell her that you'll collect the rent in person on the first. Don't wait for her to drop the rent under your door!

Likewise, if your tenant habitually pays late or has to be approached each month for the rent, you would be well advised to change your payment structure so you collect the rent in person on the first. This will save you a lot of aggravation.

If your tenant tells you she doesn't know when she will be able to pay the rent this month, pin her down. Press her to give you a date when she can pay and press her to give you something now. Think of yourself as a bill collector—and use the techniques they use.

If the promised date arrives and you still don't have the check for the rent, you should, first, count to ten, and then promptly issue a notice of termination of the tenancy, a "notice to quit" for nonpayment of rent. Even if your tenant is well-intentioned you have no choice but to assert the gravity of the situation. Your notice of termination transcends the casual relationship you may have had up to this point with your tenant.

In general, when the rent is five days late, you are entitled to send your tenant a "notice to quit" which terminates the tenancy at the end of the next rental period. For instance, if on the fifth of June your tenant has still not given you the rent for June, you could send a notice to quit so that the premises are vacated by the first of July, presuming you collected the last month's rent at the commencement of the tenancy. If you didn't collect the last month's rent, then your notice to quit will tell the tenant to get out in fourteen days. Check with your local housing court about any regulations that may apply in your area.

Clearly, the possibility that your tenant might turn out to be a deadbeat or run into some economic tough times shows the importance of requiring both a security deposit and the last month's rent, as well as of checking references.

WHEN THE RENT CHECK BOUNCES

Most people have had a check bounce at some point in their financial career, or so common wisdom dictates. Is that why it's so easy to excuse tenants whose rent check bounces?

A bounced rent check is as bad as the absence of any rent check at all. It is a breach of contract, and in many states a bounced check is considered a form of larceny—goods (in this case, your apartment) have been "stolen." Thus, you should not treat a bounced check lightly, any more than a tenant would treat lightly a landlord who shuts off the heat.

Even though Jim, your tenant, has demonstrated his good intentions by "paying you" the rent on the first, when his rent check bounces he has technically, and literally, not paid the rent. Until he has rectified the situation, Jim is borrowing from you; and remember, as in the case of the tenant who didn't pay the rent, you are not in the business of providing credit.

There are two ways you will find out your tenant's check bounced, either from your bank directly or from your tenant. Your tenant finds out before your bank does—his bank will notify him that his check is being returned to your bank, which notifies you and debits your account—and thus should notify you promptly. Clearly, you're not going to feel too kindly toward any tenant whose check bounces, but you have to respect the tenant who comes forward and lets you know right away. Conversely, if you have to call your tenant yourself and tell him that his check bounced, you'll feel even less kindly.

Whether you find out from your bank or from your tenant, handle the situation in the same way. First of all, even if you sense your tenant made a simple bookkeeping error, you have to act to protect your interests and to make sure your financial security isn't jeopardized. No matter that Jim has been with you for two years and has never had a check bounce before. Chances are his bouncing a check has thrown you into a financial tailspin

—since you've found him so reliable in the past, you may even, upon receiving his check, have written checks for the mortgage, utilities and heat. In other words, don't take any risks in collecting the overdue rent: insist on cash or a cashier's check to replace the bounced check. This will give you full use of the money immediately, (many banks put a seven- or fourteen-day hold on any checks). Immediacy is important because you're probably at least a week into the month by the time you find out about the bounced check. This way you can immediately write checks on the money or at the very least earn interest on it. Your tenant may look at you with mournful eyes when you insist on cash or a cashier's check, as if to say, "You don't trust me anymore." He's right.

Insist that your tenant pay any charges imposed on you by your bank. In addition, if one of the terms of your tenancy stipulates that you will charge for bounced checks, make sure you receive this at the same time your tenant gives you the overdue rent.

You may want to institute a new policy in the future: that the rent will be paid by cashier's check. This really depends on your judgment of the situation. Frankly, you'd be well advised to eliminate the risk of another bounced check and switch to cashier's checks. It's really not that much more trouble for your tenant, and it will set your mind at ease. Your tenant may protest and accuse you of being unduly harsh. Compare yourself to the corner grocery store: chances are if you bounced a check at Joe's Market, you'd never be able to write a check there again. However, Joe won't throw you out of the store or prohibit you from buying anything in his store: Joe will tell you, "In God we trust; all others pay cash."

If, however, you decide to continue to accept Jim's personal check, you should make it clear to him that there's a good chance you will go directly to his bank to cash it rather than depositing it. This should instill enough caution and diligence in your tenant to ensure that what happened never happens again.

Should you issue the tenant a notice to quit for nonpayment of rent instead of accepting a new payment? Certainly you have this option, and you should probably use it if your tenant has bounced more than one check. Let's face it, if you can't count on your tenant paying in a reliable fashion, you and your tenant have a nearly nonexistent business relationship.

Also, most states allow a tenant to receive only one such notice in a twelve-month period and pay the overdue rent to reinstate the tenancy. Thus, even if you plan to accept the tenant's money for the month, you might just as well issue a letter of nonpayment so that if the problem recurs you will be on solid ground should you want to evict the tenant.

Incidentally, be sure to hold on to the bounced check or make a photocopy of it (front and back) before returning it to your tenant.

NOISE

You and your tenants have the right to the quiet enjoyment of your respective apartments. Excessive noise—loud music, shouting, banging, slamming doors—on the part of one of your tenants violates this right and, if loud enough, enters the realm of criminal actions by technically disturbing the peace. As the landlord, you are obligated to prevent or stop such disturbances so that other tenants and your neighbors may continue to enjoy their peace and quiet.

If your tenant has his stereo blaring, your first step should be to evaluate the situation. Has this tenant lived in the house for three years and never been a problem up to now? Or has he just moved in? If so, you'll want to strike while the iron is hot, for two reasons. First, you'll want to establish that you consider his stereo excessively loud (and, if you've followed the suggestions earlier in this book, you will have included a noise prohibition in the written tenancy). If you wait to say anything, your tenant may assume the volume is quite acceptable, the mistake will be repeated, and a pattern will develop. Second, if you decide to say something to your tenant when you run into him in the hall, the tenant might minimize just how loud the music was. For instance, he might apologize but say, "I didn't think it was that loud. Hmmm."

The second step in dealing with a noise problem is to decide if it is a direct violation of house rules. If your ground rules specify that all parties must end at 2 A.M. and your watch says 3:00 but you can hear music, dancing and loud voices, then you're on solid ground: not only is the party noisy (which might be debatable since it is subjective), but it is going on after agreed-upon hours (which is an objective criterion).

Next, you have to decide how to proceed. Should you knock on the tenant's door and directly confront him? Should you pick up the telephone and call him? There really isn't any right or wrong answer, but you should keep two things in mind in deciding what to do next. First, gauge the likelihood of your being injured by the tenant if you confront him directly. Your happy-go-lucky tenant may turn into a pumpkin after he's had a few beers! Frankly, if it's three o'clock in the morning, you probably would do well, unless you feel like getting dressed, to call your tenant on the phone. You thus avoid embarrassing him in front of his friends, don't violate his right to privacy, save yourself a trip in case he doesn't hear you at the door, and save yourself from his wisecracks or arguments.

Whether you go down in person or call him, keep your message simple. Keep to the facts of time and place—for instance, "It's 3 A.M., the music is so loud I can hear it upstairs. I must insist you cease your festivities." If, on the other hand, the noise isn't occurring during the "quiet hours" agreed on as a term of the tenancy but simply during the evening, you could afford to be a bit more jovial about it, maybe adding, "Gee, it's great you all seem to be having such a good time—it's so loud upstairs I can't hear the water running . . ." One landlord we know was particularly creative in dealing with his two women tenants' first party—he went downstairs at 11:30 P.M., wrench in hand, and told them he would hate to throw a wrench in the works but he would have to ask them to keep it down!

Three caveats in dealing with noisy tenants. First, don't apologize for requesting quiet—if anyone should apologize, let it be the tenants. Second, don't raise your voice (unless you have to in order to be heard). Third, don't argue about the level of noise. If your tenants think you are being unreasonable they can look elsewhere for a place to live.

Although you certainly don't have to offer your tenants an explanation (I can't sleep, I have a busy day tomorrow) or offer a compromise solution, these should be considered, especially if you sense the noise results from a tenant's ignorance. For example, let's say Jim slams his front door every time he leaves the house. Clearly you and he have different standards about how to close a door properly. In an effort to be diplomatic, you might approach him and ask if the door sticks because you notice he slams it every time he leaves. If the answer is no, ask if you could look at it. Examine the door. Tell him you think it's in good working order. Close it yourself a few times. Quietly. Then, tell your tenant you expect him to close it that way from now on. Close by saying you hope he'll pay attention to this detail because it's not good for the door itself, the hinges and the door frame to be subjected to such force, and you would hate to see it damaged.

Sometimes it's helpful to be more reasonable than you have to be. If Jim has a musical instrument—an organ, for instance—that turns out to be a problem, offer him the chance to use it when no one else is home. Naturally, if you all work the same hours, your compromise solution won't help him out, but it shows you to be a reasonable landlord.

If your tenant continues to be noisy, you have to ask yourself if he is deliberately acting contrary to the terms of the tenancy. No matter how cordial your relationship has been with him thus far, it's possible you're heading for some rocky times ahead. Rather than approaching him directly again, send him a letter (certified or registered) telling him he is, in essence, violating the terms of his tenancy with you. This will put him on notice that you will not tolerate violations of your right and the right of your other tenants to the private enjoyment of your apartment. At the bottom of the letter you might write something reassuring, such as "I thought we were back on track, Sam, and didn't want to have to tell you twice that your party was unacceptably noisy."

If the noise persists, don't forget that you have several other options available, all of which are extreme and all to be reserved for extreme situations since they create hard feelings and increase the tension level in the house. If the tenant is being extremely noisy at a very late hour and you're afraid of confronting him, you can call the police on the grounds of his disturbing the peace. You should keep in mind that, just as the police don't like to get involved in domestic squabbles, they don't like to come between landlord and tenant. However, this solution may be the only way to quell the disturbance and protect your property.

If your tenant persists in being noisy but is otherwise a fine tenant (does such a tenant exist?), you can have a restraining order issued against him at the housing court in the city or town in which you live. This is, of course, not a pleasant prospect, but it may be just what the tenant needs to realize that you are serious in your concern about noise. Usually such restraining orders are temporary, for ten days' duration. During the ten-day period, you and the tenant will have to go to court and will have the opportunity to reach an amicable agreement.

If you have reached the end of your rope with your tenant, then you really have no choice but to issue a notice terminating the tenancy. For your own sanity, you may wish to have a restraining order issued simultaneously so that you can spend the next month in peace.

So far, we've covered a fairly benign albeit irritating noise problem. You may encounter a noise problem that really demands your immediate attention: you hear your tenants screaming at each other or at their children. On the simplest level, they probably aren't people with whom you want to continue sharing your home. In addition, you may have real concerns about the health and safety of some of the occupants and you certainly don't want to be negligent. (You probably cannot be held liable for any injuries a tenant suffers at the hands of another tenant or of a tenant's guests, but you definitely don't want assault or child abuse on your conscience.)

You have two choices, neither of them appealing. Either you can attempt to intervene or you can call the police. If you go for the "do it yourself" approach, be careful and try to bring a witness (of the opposite sex if you are male). You might begin your conversation by saying, "The substance of your argument is not my business, but you have made the argument my business by being so loud. I'll have to insist that you cease." If there are children in the house, you should inquire after their welfare: "Is Tony here too?" If you have any reason to believe one of your tenants is inflicting physical harm on any of the other occupants, *call the police.* When the police arrive, go down to see what is going on. After tempers cool down, tell your tenants you didn't like having to call the police, that you feel sorry for them and hope they will seek professional help, but that they are no longer welcome in your home and you will send them a written notice of termination. Then do it.

STEPPING IN BETWEEN TWO TENANTS

You may get along fine with your tenants, but perhaps your tenants don't get along with each other. Often, the complaints you might have about a tenant are the same ones that one tenant will have about the other. These include bickering over parking places, abuse of common facilities, noise, placement of trash and garbage, and pet-related complaints (the dog is noisy/smells, etc.). Sometimes the issues don't affect you directly—for instance, noise from your first-floor tenant might bother the second-floor tenant but won't necessarily waft its way up to your suite on the top floor.

Usually, by the time any dispute between tenants comes to your attention, enough resentment or peevishness will have built up between your tenants that a prompt solution is required. You may wish you had the wisdom of King Solomon when you are deciding how to handle the dispute. There are two schools of thought about how to handle this kind of hassle: one is to let the tenants solve their own problems and the other is to establish yourself as a go-between. We're in favor of the latter; tenants shouldn't have to confront one another. The dispute *is* your business by the time you're aware of it, and your involvement may very well prevent matters from unduly escalating. Also, it's likely that the disruptive tenant is doing something that violates your tenancy agreement, whether it's your noise clause, your pet clause or whatever. If that's the case, it's not just that one tenant is doing something to annoy another but that one tenant is committing an infraction that happens to annoy another tenant.

Your role here is a double one: first, to remedy the situation, and second, to smooth things over to avoid resentment and hard feelings.

Before you do anything to actively remedy the problem, be sure you have heard both sides of the story. In other words, tread softly—you don't want to get all fired up as the result of one tenant's pickiness. If one tenant comes to you on Thursday and says, "Tuesday night the people upstairs were jumping up and down or something," you'd be wise to suggest that the complaining tenant come to you promptly the next time it happens so you can see for yourself what the problem is—and if it indeed exists. Don't act on hearsay; be fair and objective.

Sometimes you'll run into tenants who seem to thrive on infighting. Every other day they will come running to you to tattle on a perceived infraction committed by another tenant. While you certainly want to encourage your tenants to come to you when they are having a problem, you don't need busybodies and it would be in your best interest to tell such tenants to relax. You could say something along the lines of "Gee, Jim, I appreciate your coming to tell me that Steve has been slamming doors upstairs from you, but we all do have to get along in the house and I think you're being overly sensitive to this particular issue."

IMPROVEMENTS OR ALTERATIONS MADE
WITHOUT YOUR PERMISSION

Most landlords specifically prohibit tenants from making improvements or alterations to the apartments without the landlord first giving express permission. Some landlords even request that their tenants secure written permission before making any improvements. The area of improvements/alterations is one of the most highly charged issues between landlords and tenants. Tenants, on the one hand, want to transform their apartment into a home, while the landlord as the owner reserves the right to insist that tenants keep the apartment in the same condition they rented it. The possibility that your tenants will make unauthorized improvements is one excellent reason to collect a security deposit.

Most tenants who make alterations without the landlord's permission aren't being deliberately malicious. Repeat this sentence three times to yourself the first time you see what liberties tenants have taken with your apartment or when you are handed a rent check that deducts the cost of the materials. Usually tenants are lackadaisical and will plead naïveté by saying, "Oh, I know you said if we painted we would have to get your permission, but I didn't think you would mind if we installed built-in bookshelves/sanded the floors/put up wallpaper/installed wall-to-wall carpeting/put up cabinets." Expect other excuses, too: your tenants will tell you they tried to find you to get your permission but that you were out of town, or that the great "special" on paint/shelves/carpeting at a store fifty miles away was only good through the end of the week.

The first step, whether you catch your tenants in the act or see the finished result during a routine inspection, is to decide whether their handiwork improves or damages the apartment. You'll have to think fast. If your tenants are in the process of painting and are doing an adequate job, you probably should let them finish. If, on the other hand, you really don't like the color choice, you can tell your tenants to go ahead and finish but that they will have to paint the apartment the original color before they move out; this is what's known as demanding that "the premises be restored to their original condition." If your tenants are doing an unsatisfactory job, you certainly don't want to let them continue. Tell them you're not pleased that they are doing unauthorized painting, that you're not pleased with their progress so you'll have to insist that they cease, and that you'll have to hire painters to finish the job. If they have been good tenants up to this point, you will want to sound reasonable. After all, you're going to have to continue living in the same house together, so it won't do you any good to be harsh.

Sometimes you first find out about unauthorized alterations when your tenants deduct the cost of materials from their rent check or knock on your door and hand you receipts for materials. In the case of a deducted check, you should hand it back to your tenant and ask for a check for the rent. If you accept it and deposit it, you are in fact accepting the check and thus accepting the alteration and your tenant's charges. Likewise, hand any receipts back to your tenant with a firm but polite "No."

Never, ever, reimburse a tenant for the cost of unauthorized alterations—regardless of whether or not they in fact improve the apartment or not. Your tenants will infer that you have approved the alterations if you pay for them; paying for them amounts to your tacit acceptance. Be prepared, however, to quarrel with your tenants over this, particularly if the alterations ultimately make the apartment more marketable—your tenants will tell you you're being unfair and unreasonable, or they'll protest that you can claim the expense on your income tax and they can't, that you said you would pay for paint and if they had gotten your permission you would pay for it. You certainly can agree with them on these points, but stick to your guns—their failure to get permission should be considered a serious infraction.

What should you do if, in your opinion, the alterations damage the value of the apartment? You can make the tenants themselves restore the apartment immediately to its original condition, or you can hire someone to do it. Also, you can wait until the tenants move out to have it done. The tenants, however, should always be the ones to pay for the work. If you have it done immediately, you'd be wise to bill the tenants directly rather than waiting until they move out and deducting the cost from the security deposit. It's not a good idea to reduce the amount of the security deposit during the course of the tenancy; you'll want to have the maximum deposit in reserve for future unforeseen damage. However, if for some reason—let's say the cost to restore the apartment to original condition isn't going to be substantial—you decide to deduct the amount later, send your tenants a registered letter confirming this. If they don't move out for several years, they may not remember the exact terms of your agreement. Likewise, if your tenants are going to wait until the end of the tenancy to do the actual work themselves, it would be a good idea to send them a letter, again by registered mail, confirming that this will be done but that if they don't do it themselves you will deduct it from their deposit. Thus, if your tenants have put up some shelf brackets in the living room, you may opt to leave them up, but upon their moving insist that the walls will have to be spackled and touched up.

In rare instances, the extent, nature and quality of alterations will be so extensive and unacceptable that you may choose the most extreme solution available to you and decide to begin eviction proceedings. Fortunately, though, you won't run up against this very often!

DAMAGE TO THE PREMISES

You have to expect a certain amount of wear and tear in the apartment. In fact, standard leases are careful to differentiate between "wear and tear" and "damage." Scuff marks on the floors are wear and tear, deep scratches are damage. Fingerprints on the wall constitute wear and tear; large gouges in the plaster are damage. Pet stains and broken windows or locks are damage. Wear and tear is considered the landlord's responsibility, whereas damage is the tenant's responsibility.

Recouping the cost to repair damage should be handled in the same way as alterations. That is, bill your tenant directly as it comes up, rather than waiting and deducting the cost from the security deposit.

What about willful damage? What should you do if you discover your tenants have been putting cigarettes out on the floor, punching holes in the wall or throwing things at the ceiling? This is clearly unacceptable, inexcusable behavior on the part of unacceptable tenants—you should move quickly to evict them unless you want to risk further serious damage. Don't feel sorry for your tenants or try to be their psychiatrist; of course they must be somewhat unbalanced or have a violent temper or *something* to have caused such serious damage, but you really don't want such tenants to continue living there, do you?

Don't waste a minute—delays could jeopardize your apartment and your ability to re-rent it. First, immediately issue a notice of termination of the tenancy if your tenants are tenants at will. If your tenants have a lease, you probably can still give thirty days' notice provided your lease has a clause in it about damage.

Next, go down to your city or town's housing court and get a restraining order issued to prevent your tenants from continuing the damage. Even if you have confronted your tenants and they have agreed to stop damaging the premises, you should get the order anyway. A restraining order is a marvelous tool you can use to protect your rights. Although it involves a trip to the courthouse, file a formal complaint and prepare a written affidavit citing what the problem is. At the bottom of your affidavit, you will fill in what your requested "relief" is, and it is here that you would write "Prevent Jim Tenant from kicking walls" or "Prevent Carol Tenant from extinguishing cigarettes on floor." The judge will review it and will either issue a temporary restraining order (good for ten days but subject to being extended) or request a "show case" hearing which both you and your tenant will have to attend. At such a hearing, you will have to "show" why you want such a restraining order issued. Usually, a tenant who is willfully damaging your apartment will be brought to his or her senses upon being served with a restraining order.

You probably will want to get a restraining order only when you want to terminate a tenancy. You can be sure a restraining order will not wed you forever to a tenant's heart!

Next, you should get a written appraisal of the cost of repairing the damage and send a copy to your tenant. Have the damage repaired and bill your tenant for it.

Fortunately, most tenants treat their apartment with care and respect. But the mere possibility that your tenants might, willfully or otherwise, damage their apartment underlines the importance of requesting a security deposit and to request the maximum amount allowed by law.

FAILURE TO KEEP UP TO YOUR STANDARDS

Let's say Jim's apartment comes with a yard or small patio and you've specified in his tenancy agreement that he's responsible for cutting the grass, weeding the garden, raking the leaves, and otherwise keeping the space tidy. A month goes by and the grass gets as long as your temper grows short. You have three choices: say nothing and hope your tenant will have a spontaneous remission; ask the tenant to do routine upkeep on a specified schedule, such as once every two weeks; and, last, change the terms of the tenancy so that the responsibility is yours. Your first option may keep your tenant happy but will give you an ulcer. Your second option *may* work if your tenant is motivated. Your third option is your best bet. Our experience indicates that a tenant whose standards are at great odds with yours will never—repeat, never—measure up. Your yard will never look the way you want it to; the patio will always look worn around the edges. You'll get far fewer gray hairs if you do it yourself. In this case, if you had set the rent to compensate the tenant for his efforts, you should, of course, adjust it (upward, ho!).

PET-RELATED PROBLEMS

If you allow pets and have followed the advice given in Chapter 7, then you have already stipulated that having a pet is conditional on the pet's behavior. If the pet misbehaves—whether it barks, scratches, smells, or goes into heat on a regular basis—you should act quickly to correct the problem. If you decide after six months of hearing your downstairs neighbors' dog bark that you just can't take it any more, you'll be on shaky ground. By this time you may be attached to your tenants, your tenants are quite attached to their dog, and they will justifiably wonder why it took you so long to mention it. Also, if you wait that long, chances are you'll be so annoyed at this point that you'll have lost perspective.

Fortunately, most pet problems have solutions that will allow your tenants to keep their pet. Some of the solutions may be contrary to the way your tenants would like to raise their pet, but at least you are offering them the option of keeping their pet and keeping the apartment.

Here are some common problems, which break down into two indisputable areas: either the pet is damaging the apartment in some way or it is behaving in a way that makes you or the other tenants complain. (When you approach the tenants, keep in mind that you allowed the pet on a conditional basis, that not all apartments allow pets, and that you really should require a security deposit if you do not already. If you have pets yourself, you might be in the position to offer some genuine tips—for example, about the type of cat litter you've found most effective against odor, etc.)

- The dog or cat is in heat and attracts all the neighborhood male dogs. The solution to this one is easy: require that the dog or cat be fixed.
- The male cat sprays. Again, the tenants should get the cat fixed (although there's no guarantee that this will work).
- The dog barks all day long when the tenants are away. The solution is a twofold one. First, require that the dog be muzzled to prevent this obnoxious behavior. Contrary to what some dog lovers would have you believe, muzzling is neither cruel nor painful for a dog. If your tenants balk, remind them that you are suggesting this as a choice: they either muzzle or get rid of the dog. Second, you might suggest that the tenants try training the dog—either through obedience school or on their own—not to bark when they leave.
- The cat litter smells so bad you can smell it two floors up. First, ask the tenants how often they change the box. Then, tell the tenants that the odor is offensive and suggest that they change it more frequently.
- The dog or cat urinates on the floor, staining it. First of all, try to determine if this was an isolated incident—for instance, the pet might be sick. If so, you're in luck. If, however, it results from poor training, you'll have to monitor the situation with vigilance—constant piddling not only stains but seeps into the floor or carpet, so much so that the odor is almost impossible to remove. If the incident is repeated, you will probably have

to insist that either the tenants or the pet move. In any case, the tenants will have to pay for any damage that the pet has caused.

- The dog scratches or chews on the woodwork. The solution to this one isn't easy for tenants to accept. Unless you want to replace your doors, moldings and windowsills when the tenants move out, you'll have to insist that Fido find a new home.
- The dog or cat has fleas. Unfortunately for the tenants, you probably discovered that their pet has fleas when you discovered fleas in your petless apartment. These are relatively easy to get rid of—insist on the pet's wearing a flea collar and getting flea baths and ask the tenants to set off a "flea bomb," available at most hardware stores. You might want to stipulate, if your state allows you to, that you will return the pet deposit after forty-five days. As one Southern landlord told us, "We sometimes can't determine whether there are fleas or not until someone new moves in . . . We keep the pet deposit until the apartment has been occupied for four to six weeks by a new tenant."
- The dog or cat gets into the trash before it is picked up by the garbage collectors. The solution to this one is easy: ask the tenants to keep their pet indoors until the trash is picked up.

WHEN YOUR TENANT WANTS TO BE FRIENDS

In no other small business or investment do you run as much of a risk of becoming too friendly with the integral part of the business. In the same way that people are advised not to do business with friends, you're advised not to be friends with the people you're doing business with—your tenants. Some landlords and tenants disagree with this mode of behavior, but the consequences of being buddies with your tenants are many, most of them unpleasant. If and when the time comes for you to raise the rent or terminate the tenancy, or if some unforeseen problem arises between you and your tenants, it will be very difficult for you to maintain a professional and objective stance.

The thing to keep in mind is that the landlord-tenant relationship takes precedence over any potential friendship—it's comparable to an employer-employee relationship. You and your boss may be very close, but your boss does have more of a say about your life than you do about his. The same holds true for a landlord-tenant relationship. You're privy to the tenants' financial affairs if you had them fill out a detailed application, can determine how much their rent is, and in fact can determine where they live! Your tenants, on the other hand, know only what you tell them and what is a matter of public record (yes, they can find out your taxes, purchase price and amount of your mortgage!). While some landlords make it a practice to sit down with their tenants and share information about their financial affairs, this is not recommended except under rare circumstances. You can never really, ever take off your landlord hat—until your tenants move. In fact, a number of landlords we know have become friends with their tenants—after they move out.

All this is not to say you can't be cordial. But you should keep your distance—invite your tenants in for a drink over the holidays, offer your tenants some fresh tomatoes from your garden, inquire after their health, their new job, their children's activities. Naturally, too, if both of you have children, encourage them to be friends but be careful that your child doesn't spend too much time in your tenants' apartment.

What should you do about a tenant who is overly nosy or lonely? You return home from work and invariably around 7 P.M. your tenant knocks on the door and says, "Got a minute?/ By the way, a delivery man came/Could I paint the bedroom/ The neighbor's dog dug up your garden/Sally from downstairs bugs me . . ." Unless you want to encourage such a daily exchange, you should tactfully discourage your tenants from bothering you. First of all, don't invite your tenants in—you may have trouble getting them out. Try to keep the conversation brief and to the point. Find out what they want and then look for a way to end the conversation. Some tried and true excuses are: "I've got to walk the dog/turn off the broiler/turn off the tub/ feed the baby/watch the news/meet someone in fifteen minutes . . . I am expecting company/am on the phone/have had a hard day/must start dinner . . ." You don't have to be too blunt—you could even say, "Gee, Carol, thanks for letting me know that. Was there anything else?" You don't, of course, want her to refrain from telling you when something is wrong, so you should be as pleasant as can be—you merely want to discourage idle chitchat.

If a tenant persists in knocking on your door on a daily basis, you may have to be a bit more direct and say, "Gee, Carol, every night this week you've had some question, problem or complaint. Is something else on your mind? If not, I'd really prefer to be able to come home and relax. Why don't you save your questions so that we can touch base on several things at once? Naturally, though, don't hesitate to come down if it's serious." This should keep away even the meddlesome tenant.

WHEN YOUR TENANT GETS A NEW
ROOMMATE OR SUBLETS

No one likes surprises—nor will you, the landlord, like bumping into a total stranger in your own house. Chances are your "ground rules" specified that your tenant would have to have permission before subletting or getting a roommate; you should always reserve the right to determine who will live in your house. Thus, if you encounter a stranger in the hall, you will probably assume it's just a visitor. However, perhaps the stranger introduces herself by saying, "Hi, I'm Sarah Wishful. What a fabulous house!" You should count to ten and then try to determine if she has in fact moved in.

Several other things may lead you to think that someone new has moved in. Perhaps there are two cars parked out front every night for three weeks, or you hear the television on in your tenant's apartment when you know you just saw her leave for work.

The first thing to do is to find out if in fact someone new has moved in. Be direct about it and ask your original tenant. Don't be accusatory until you have the whole story. You might say, "Gee, Jim, do you have someone visiting for a while? I only ask because it surprised me to see someone going in and out of your apartment when you were out this week." If he says, "Oh, that's Sarah; she and I are living together now," you should always let the tenant know you reserve the right to determine who lives in the house. You might say, if you approve in principle of the new tenant, "Jim, that's great. I will of course want to have Sarah fill out an application," (you want to know if Sarah could pay the rent if Jim then moved out) "and if it checks out," (again, apply the same techniques you used to find Jim in the first place—you don't want a deadbeat on your hands) "we can rewrite the tenancy so that she's included."

Occasionally, the new roommate or subletting tenant won't be acceptable—possibly it's someone who can't part with his frisky and noisy dog or her three toddlers (and the apartment is a studio). You may be in the position of having to tell your original tenant that everyone will have to move. But don't do it unless you mean it. Be reasonable; don't expect them to move out overnight (even though they moved in overnight!) but do set a date by which time they must be out. Incidentally, if your tenant pays the rent during the time the new roommate is living there, be sure to give the tenant a receipt which indicates that you have not allowed the new roommate to stay. Otherwise, your acceptance of the rent money could be construed as acceptance of a new tenant.

> Dear Jim Tenant:
> This acknowledges receipt of your check #123 in the amount of $350.00 for the June rent. However, as we discussed, Sarah Wishful is not a tenant and will move out by the end of the month. Thanks.
>
> Yours sincerely,
>
> Carol Landlord

If you get into a tussle with your original tenant about it, remember that you have a trump card to play if you so desire: you can always terminate the tenancy so that everyone has to move out. Incidentally, unless you plan to end the tenancy, in the case of a recalcitrant couple there's really no point in telling your tenant that the new roommate has to move. If you lose your nerve and finally consent to the new person moving in, it may be difficult to be firm on other issues.

If you allow a new tenant to move in, you should request an application and rewrite the rental agreement to reflect the new situation.

WHEN YOUR TENANT MAKES EXCESSIVE REQUESTS

When you reach your limit (trust your instincts—when you think you've reached it, you have!), say, "Jim, we're not going to do that, and in fact we think your apartment is dandy. We don't plan to do any—repeat, any—more to it for another six months." Then stick to it. Otherwise you will go mad.

WHEN YOUR TENANT'S APARTMENT IS A MESS

Let's say your new tenant moved in six months ago and you discover cockroaches, mice, a general disarray or an accumulation of mold and filth in her apartment. This is a tricky situation because it involves telling your tenant she's a slob. If you decide you have to get the apartment fumigated, you could tell her it's something you do annually. If, on the other hand, the place is a mess, you should be sure you collected a security deposit and also tell her you expect her to keep the apartment tidier. No one can argue with mold and mildew! One landlord we know even went so far as to spend a Saturday with his bachelor tenant, showing him how to clean a toilet, sink and tub. Another subtly suggested that his tenant get a cleaning woman to come in once a week—since the landlord had one, too, the suggestion was taken in the right spirit.

WHEN YOU RENT OUT A ROOM IN YOUR HOME

Some of the hassles you may encounter if you rent out a room in your home won't be encountered by other types of landlords. They usually involve some misappropriation of the space and are almost always impossible to ignore.

- *Your tenant hogs the telephone.* Once you discover you've rented a room to the city's most popular social butterfly, it's time to place restrictions on his use of the phone (e.g., no calls over five minutes, calls only between 9 P.M. and 10 P.M.—whenever you don't anticipate getting or making calls) or insist that the tenant get his own phone installed. The latter is recommended if you feel it's really a problem—simply tell Jim Tenant that you've missed several important calls and think it would be simpler if he had his own phone.

- *Your tenant insists on coming into your personal rooms.* If you're lucky, you have set aside some private space in your home that you reserve for your exclusive use. Even if you make it clear that your tenant is not welcome in that space, the bored or meddling tenant will try to intrude, usually on the pretense that he has a question or problem. If it's a problem that can't be resolved in a matter of a few seconds, leave your space and get comfortable in the public space (living room, kitchen, etc.). In the process, even say something along the lines of "Come on, Jim, let's go out of my room to discuss this." If he stops by merely to chat, you may have to be right to the point and say, "Jim, I'd like to be alone now—would you be so good as to close the door on your way out?" If you come home some day and find your tenant curled up in your favorite bedroom chair, you should without fail tell your tenant that your rooms are for your exclusive use and that finding him in them again will be grounds for eviction.

- *Your tenant and you butt heads in the kitchen.* As one long-time landlord says, "The kitchen is a big bone of contention with people who live in your house. Both eating and cleaning." Whatever your arrangements are, the kitchen is potentially an area of conflict. Your tenant eats your food, doesn't clean up after himself, or hangs around while you cook dinner for your family and offers suggestions about how to make Shrimp Creole. If you haven't laid out clear ground rules you'll live to regret it. Since you can't in good conscience revoke kitchen privileges, it's incumbent on you to spell out your preferred policy or to change the policy somewhat.

For example, one couple put an elastic band around any noncommunal food in the refrigerator and let each tenant have an individual cabinet. This system quickly was put to use after one of the tenants helped himself to half of an apple pie that was being saved for an in-law's pending visit.

As good fences make good neighbors, clear ground rules make happy housemates.

11

Terminating the Tenancy

Tenants move out under one of two conditions—the move is either voluntary or involuntary. Bear in mind that there's no difference in the end result: you regain your apartment and begin the cycle of interviewing, screening, interviewing and selecting tenants. The procedures in both cases are basically the same; however, they will seem worlds apart because of the acrimony that enters in when you terminate the tenancy.

When you receive notice from a good tenant or decide it is time to terminate the tenancy of a less satisfactory tenant, don't waste a lot of time wondering what could have been different so that your tenant had stayed or so that "things wouldn't have ended up here." If you are a landlord, you have to accept the fact that you will have very few "lifelong" tenants. Also, if you are not inhibited by rent control, look upon vacancies as a chance to command more rent for the apartment and as an opportunity to make needed improvements. If your model tenants have given notice, why not take this opportunity to thank them and ask if they would spread the word among their friends that the apartment is available. You could even consider offering them half a month's rent as "finder's fee" if anyone referred by them rents the apartment and stays six months.

GROUNDS FOR TERMINATION

If you wish to terminate a tenant's tenancy, be sure you follow the local statutes precisely. As mentioned elsewhere in this book, laws protecting tenants have multiplied. If you're about to terminate a tenancy, the last thing you need is to have your tenant or a housing court judge toss out or delay your case on a technicality. This is not the time to be casual—don't knock on Jim's door and say to him, "Things aren't working out so I'm going to have to ask you to leave." If you are ending a tenancy, put it in writing and do so in accordance with your local statute. The first time you terminate a tenancy you should consult a lawyer or housing court clerk to ensure you are following the correct procedures.

Under what circumstances would you terminate a tenancy? Again, you should check your local housing court or statutes to be sure your grounds are legitimate, but in general, the grounds for termination or nonrenewal of a lease are as follows:

— you need the apartment for your personal use or for your immediate family;
— your tenant has failed to pay the rent;
— your tenant has violated a substantial obligation of the tenancy;
— your tenant has used the apartment for immoral or illegal purposes;
— the apartment is not used as the tenant's primary residence;
— your tenant will not allow you to enter the apartment in an emergency or to make repairs or to show the apartment to a prospective purchaser, or will not allow you to enter to inspect the premises;
— your tenant is committing a nuisance to you or other tenants;
— you are converting your house to condominiums or cooperative apartments;
— your tenant's occupancy subjects you to a criminal penalty;
— you need the apartment for your business;
— your house is being taken by eminent domain;

— there are hazardous or dangerous conditions, the repair of which does not permit occupancy;
— your building is—alas—being demolished; or
— either landlord or tenant dies.

Incidentally, you may not terminate the tenancy because your tenant is active in a tenants' group, is attempting to organize other tenants, or has reported actual or perceived violations of the sanitary code or housing codes to an official agency—tempting though it may be to rid yourself of someone who might "cause trouble." Unfortunately, most tenants know what your limitations are and may use the law against you. For example, let's say Jim Tenant has four roommates move into his one-bedroom apartment. The noise is driving you crazy, as is your mounting water bill. Jim may sense this and call in the housing inspector, who finds two minor violations. Jim is pretty well protected for the time being from any eviction proceedings you may initiate. Even though he is in violation of one of the terms of his lease, he will probably be able to stay in the apartment (but without his new roommates) until the code violations are fixed.

TERMINATION PROCEDURE

What, though, are the general steps you would take to terminate a tenancy? They are as follows:

1. Give proper notice, as dictated by the laws in your community
2. Give your tenant a receipt for the last month's rent
3. Inspect the premises
4. Get the tenant's forwarding address
5. Inspect the premises after your tenant has moved
6. Return the security deposit, once you have determined that there is no damage.

It's important to take termination step by step, as it's easy to get caught up in the problems at hand. For instance, if your tenant falls behind in the rent, you may be so frazzled by this unexpected development (to say nothing of being poorer as the result of it) that you miss some crucial ingredient. Also, until your tenant actually moves, you are going to be understandably anxious over the possibility that your tenant will ignore, question or challenge the termination notice, damage the premises, or otherwise make the process a slower and more unpleasant one for all concerned. This anxiety can lead you to do something silly—thus, proceed one step at a time.

A LEASE OR TENANCY AT WILL

If you have a lease and your tenant is violating one of its clauses or covenants, you should notify the tenant in writing that such a violation exists. Tenants should almost always be given the opportunity to redeem themselves before termination of the tenancy. Remember that you may not be able to terminate a lease for an insubstantial violation. Substantial violations might include pets, noise, unauthorized occupants, damage and non-payment of rent.

If you have a non-self-extending lease with your tenant, you do not need grounds for not renewing the lease. (However, in some states you must offer your tenant a new lease.) A simple note telling your tenant that the lease will not be renewed is sufficient. Again, be sure and do so in a timely fashion in compliance with any local or state laws that apply.

If you have a tenancy at will, as described in Chapter 6, you may terminate the tenancy whenever you wish (as can your tenant). You do not have to give a reason, although you may wish to if the circumstances are beyond your control.

DO YOU WANT THE RENT OR THE APARTMENT?

Generally speaking, there are two types of "notices to quit" (the premises): "Notice to Quit for Nonpayment of Rent" and "Notice to Quit for Possession." In the case of nonpayment of rent, you may send your tenant a Notice to Quit for Nonpayment of Rent as soon as the rent is overdue (you do not have to wait a grace period—check your state for length of time). In many states, tenants can redeem themselves simply by paying the back rent, and the notice usually states this. However, in many states the landlord is protected if a tenant wants to pay the rent in this late fashion on a regular basis; tenants can only redeem themselves from *one* nonpayment notice in twelve months' time. See the sample notice.

A Notice to Quit for Possession is, as implied, designed to allow you to regain possession of the apartment. It is not necessarily contingent on tenants' behavior, but many landlords (and courts) favor letting tenants redeem themselves.

When your tenant is behind in the rent, it is very important to act promptly in sending notice. If you have both the tenant's last month's rent and a security deposit, then you will not have lost any money when your tenant moves out without paying the overdue rent. If, however, you wait a month before issuing official notice, then you stand to lose at least a month's rent. Never assume that your tenants will naturally get back on track; if they miss a month's rent, it will get harder and harder for them to catch up. Also, even if you are on good terms with a tenant and know there is a good reason for the rent to be late, it is still a good idea to give the tenant an official notice that the rent is overdue. You could soften it by saying something along the lines of "I know, Jim, you told me the rent would be late, but I thought this official piece of paper would remind both of us that it's due."

One landlord we know held off giving her tenants official notice of overdue rent for several months. She had just bought the house and didn't really want to alienate the seven gypsies living in the first-floor apartment. It seemed as though they were working hard and were earnest in their promises to pay the rent. By the time she gave them an official notice, she was owed three months' rent. They did not pay the overdue rent; she moved to have them evicted, which took even more time. By the time they moved, she had lost five months' rent.

The thing to remember is that you may not receive the overdue rent and may have to initiate eviction proceedings. In most areas, you will not be able to move on to this next step until you have served the tenants a proper Notice to Quit for Nonpayment of Rent.

KEEPING GOOD RECORDS

It's important to remember to keep impeccable records during the termination process. You should, as is standard business practice, keep copies of any letters or notices you send your tenants. Also, particularly if a tenant is belligerent, keep a diary of any relevant events, including times your tenant tries to goad you on, for example, by blasting his stereo at 2 A.M. or by being careless or noisy. Finally, make a few notes about why you are terminating the tenancy, if you haven't already done so. Thinking ahead: even after your tenants move, you should keep their "file" for seven years.

PROPER NOTICE

What constitutes proper notice? As mentioned above, notice should always be in writing. If you are on reasonably amicable terms and the termination is not your tenant's fault (let's say your octogenarian grandfather wants to move in), then you could give as much notice as possible. Even when you tell your tenant verbally that this will happen, always send a written notice. Your notice of termination should include the date, a description of the premises, your name, and an end date.

NOTICE TO QUIT FOR POSSESSION

June 30, 1985

Dear Carol Tenant:

Your tenancy at will for the apartment at 186 Pacific St., Apartment 1, will be terminated at the end of the next rental period.

Please vacate the premises on or before midnight, July 31, 1985.

Sincerely,

Jim Landlord

NOTICE TO QUIT FOR NONPAYMENT OF RENT

June 2, 1985

Dear Carol Tenant:

You are hereby notified that your rent for June is overdue. You are hereby ordered to pay the full amount due within ten days. If you fail to do so you are required to quit the premises within fourteen days. If you fail to vacate, I will take legal action to evict you.

Sincerely,

Jim Landlord

NOTICE TO QUIT FOR POSSESSION
(if you have a lease)

June 17, 1985

Dear Carol Tenant:

You have violated your lease for Apartment 1, 186 Pacific Street, Smalltown, as follows:

— your waterbed is in violation of Clause 6; and

— your roommates are in violation of Clause 13.

You are hereby required to remedy this situation within seven days or quit the premises. If you fail to do so, I will take legal action to evict you.

Sincerely,

Jim Landlord

The laws in your community may dictate how notice will be served, but one of the following methods is usually recommended, so that you have proof that notice was served:

1. Send the letter to the tenant by certified mail, return receipt requested.
2. Hand your tenant the letter; if you do this, have a witness present or ask your tenant to sign a receipt for the letter.
3. Have a sheriff or constable serve the letter to the tenant.

If you sense the slightest animosity on the part of your tenant, you should have the notice served. Your tenant can refuse to accept a certified letter or could claim he did not receive the letter (strangely enough, the signed receipt does not constitute proof) or that you never gave it to him. If you are terminating the tenancy because of nonpayment, then your tenant's denial will surely lead to the eviction process and will result in more unpaid rent. Having the letter served by your local sheriff (who won't, incidentally, arrive on a horse with a badge) is relatively economical (prices range from ten to fifty dollars), considering what's at stake. It's straightforward, undeniable, and shows your tenant you mean business.

Notice of termination should be at least one full rental period; although the notice is often referred to as "thirty days' notice," this is in fact erroneous. For months that have thirty-one days, thirty-one full days are needed. For example, if you wish to have the apartment vacant on the first of September, you would have to give *thirty-two* days' notice, giving notice on July 31.

WHEN YOUR TENANT GIVES NOTICE

If your tenant gives notice, it is a good idea to give him a second receipt for his last month's rent (you would have already given him a receipt at the beginning of the tenancy). This receipt acknowledges the fact the tenancy is ending and gives you an opportunity to specify when the premises should be vacated, as the following example shows.

January 1, 1985

Dear Jim Tenant:

Since this month will be your last month at 186 Pacific Street, Apartment 1, Smalltown, we hereby apply your last month's rent as January's rent and expect you will vacate the premises by January 31, 1985.

Sincerely,

Carol Landlord

You could also use the opportunity to write a little personal note on the bottom along the lines of "Good luck in New Mexico" or "We've enjoyed having you live here."

Also, let your tenant know what he should do to deliver the premises in acceptable condition.

INSPECTING PREMISES AND RETURNING
SECURITY DEPOSIT

After notice has been given (by you or by your tenants), you should inspect the premises to gauge whether or not the apartment has suffered any damage since your tenants moved in. You will not want to return the security deposit until after your tenants have moved out (remember, delivery men brought in the refrigerator and Mediterranean-style furniture, but your tenants just informed you they intend to do all the moving themselves). Moving can cause damage. Also, there are some things that will not become evident to you until after your tenants' furniture has been removed.

If you terminated the tenancy, your tenants may not want to let you in and may in fact deny you access. Remind them that you have the legal right to inspect the premises.

After your tenant moves out, reinspect the apartment to assess the condition, comparing it to the Apartment Condition Report (see Chapter 6) which both you and your tenant signed. You should do this inspection as soon as possible. In the event there is substantial damage, you may need to get an estimate of the cost to repair it. In any case, follow the laws that govern your community regarding security deposits very carefully and precisely—this is a "hot issue" among tenants. In most areas, you have to return the security deposit within a specified amount of time, often within thirty days of the end of the tenancy.

If you do not find any damage or are not owed any unpaid rent, you would return the tenant's security deposit in full, including any interest due. Be sure to give your tenant a letter when you return it, along the lines of the following example:

LETTER RETURNING SECURITY DEPOSIT

June 30, 1985

Dear Jim Tenant:

Enclosed herewith my check #472 in the amount of $504.03, the full amount of the deposit plus the interest due thereupon, of your security deposit for 186 Pacific St., Smalltown, Apt. 1.

Sincerely,

Carol Landlord,
Landlord

You may deduct from the tenant's security deposit under the following three circumstances: when there is damage to the apartment (beyond normal wear and tear); when you are owed unpaid rent; or when you are owed an uncollected share of tax increases (if your lease or tenancy agreement allows for these). If you do make deductions from the total amount, you should itemize the charges carefully and supply your tenant with receipts.

RETURN OF SECURITY DEPOSIT, WITH DEDUCTIONS

June 30, 1985

To: Jim Tenant

Enclosed is my check #575 in the amount of $421.00, which represents your security deposit less deductions. A breakdown follows:

Total security deposit held	$500.00
Plus accrued interest	4.03
TOTAL	$504.03
Damage:	
Replace stove burner	54.03
Repair gouged plaster, livingroom	15.00
Replace brass sconce	14.00
TOTAL	$83.03

Sincerely,

Carol Landlord,
Landlord

Remember you cannot charge the tenant for "reasonable wear and tear," as described on page 188–89. Look to your local statutes for guidelines. Remember, too, that damage does not necessarily have to be deliberately caused by tenants. Whether they broke two of the shelves in the refrigerator out of spite or carelessness is not really the issue; the cost to replace them is.

On first inspection, you may feel petty as you make a few notes and cross them out. "Oh, this is ridiculous, to think of charging Jim Tenant for these scratches on the floor, the fact the apartment is really very dirty, these three broken doorknobs, this one cracked window, and that spot on the carpet." Make a full list—room by room, item by item—and calculate how much money and time each one will cost you to repair or replace. Even the smallest damage takes time and money to repair—and a full list of them could run up from two to five hundred dollars.

If the amount of damage exceeds the security deposit, you have the right to take the tenant to small claims court or to civil court if he will not pay your itemized bill.

EVICTION

Even though you can rent to anyone you want (as long as you don't discriminate by age, color, etc.), once you've rented, it is not that easy to get rid of an undesirable tenant. If you have exhausted all other resources in trying to make your tenant pay overdue rent or otherwise conform to the clauses of his lease, then you will have no choice but to initiate eviction proceedings. Eviction is your trump card as a landlord; it is a powerful tool and should not be used frivolously. Although landlords do not like to evict tenants, they should be prepared to do so when necessary.

There is no such thing as an amicable eviction. The eviction process is highly charged with emotion and acrimony. At times, eviction resembles a bitter divorce, one of the differences being that an eviction is rather like getting a divorce to end an arranged marriage because you "didn't know what you were getting." The landlord will be expected to maintain his or her composure and restraint through the process, while the tenant can behave in the most outrageous fashion. It's analogous to firing someone—your employee might yell and curse and make accusations, while you must stay calm—except that you have to live in the same house with the person you are evicting.

Without the threat of eviction hanging over even the best tenants' heads, landlords would be unable to enforce many of the covenants of the tenancy agreement. Don't forget, no matter how harassed or aggravated you feel during what may seem like an interminable eviction proceeding, eviction will enable you to regain possession of your property. You will still have your house and what you always had. You are not the one who is forced to move. Remember this, no matter how expensive the process turns out to be. Be patient, too—eviction can take up to six months, and on the average one to two months.

When should you file for an eviction? One simple way to decide is: if you ever think seriously about evicting a tenant, then you should follow your instincts and do it. Don't think for a minute that your tenant will "come around." Specifically, though, you should file for an eviction if your tenants have not paid the overdue rent by the date specified in your Notice to Quit for Nonpayment of Rent, if your tenants have not corrected the breach in the lease that prompted you to issue a Notice to Quit for Possession, if you issue a simple Notice to Quit for Possession and your tenants inform you they are not moving, or if they refuse to sign a new lease at the end of term and refuse to move.

After you have decided to initiate formal eviction proceedings, concentrate on the goal of getting your tenants out. Don't get emotional or look back. Attempt to learn from your experience with your tenants but don't play the "if only" game. Once you have initiated the proceedings, the split between you and your tenants is irrevocable.

Recognize that the road is not going to be an easy one. Expect your tenants to try every trick in the book to buy time—and "time" is all they are going to be able to buy. Depending on local regulations, chances are you will succeed in regaining possession of your apartment if you persevere. Even though laws have become increasingly pro-tenant, our society is still based on the concept of property.

What are some of the tactics your tenants may use to buy time or annoy you? They may, on receipt of the eviction notice, call the local housing inspector and point out perceived violations of the code even though they never notified you previously of same. They may request a delay for the hearing. They may claim "hardship" in finding a new place to live and be granted a "stay" for up to six months, especially if the eviction does not stem from nonpayment of rent. They may file counterclaims against you, through which they try to make you the defendant in your own house. Tenants often select from a fixed menu of counterclaims; these include harassment, invasion of privacy, interference with quiet enjoyment, emotional distress, and violation of the warranty of habitability. In addition, your tenants may claim the eviction is a retaliatory measure. Legal aid and tenants' groups, in fact, often recommend that a tenant file every possible counterclaim that may be appropriate and worry about the specifics later.

In addition to following a specific set of procedures that will be dictated by local regulations, it's advisable to cease verbal communication with your tenants. If your tenants have been behind in the rent and this is the reason for eviction, give up trying to get them to pay up. Continue to keep careful records if violations of your tenancy exist and persist. For example, if you are evicting your tenants because they have a dog without your consent, make a note recording those occasions on which the dog is loud or disruptive. Corroborate your observations by having a friend or neighbor witness the dog in question or take a photograph. If your tenants' disruptive behavior costs you money, then you should of course save all receipts and written estimates for work done; these will become part of your case against your tenants.

If you have never evicted a tenant, it is a good idea to consult a lawyer, particularly since laws in many states are decidedly pro-tenant. Many courts and judges are not sympathetic to landlords and treat apartments as tenants' consumer products instead of landlords' property. Also, because in many areas there is a critical shortage of vacant apartments, it is not infrequent for judges to attempt to "patch things up" between landlords and tenants because of tenants' reported difficulties in finding affordable space. Remember that landlord-tenant law is subject to change, which may affect your particular case. The laws regarding eviction are usually quite intricate in terms of what has to be filed, when it has to be filed, and where it has to be filed. Strict penalties may be levied against you if you are not in conformity with the law, and your case may be tossed out on a technicality or delayed for a month or more. Thus, if you're bound and determined to regain possession of your apartment, consult a lawyer. You should always consult a lawyer if a tenant makes counterclaims against you—for all of the above reasons, but also because you can almost guarantee your tenant's counterclaims were prepared with the help of a lawyer.

Consider a lawyer a scout or field guide through the bog of eviction. You have a lot at stake.

TEMPORARY RESTRAINING ORDER

If you initiate eviction proceedings because your tenant is substantially violating one of the covenants of the lease or tenancy agreement and because that violation serves to damage the apartment or jeopardize the health and safety of the occupants of the house, you may go to court and have a Temporary Restraining Order issued to prevent your tenant from continuing the objectionable behavior. This procedure could be triggered by a tenant who fails to keep the main door to the house locked, is inflicting malicious damage on the apartment, has a loud illegal pet, or has loud parties every night of the week.

"SELF-HELP" EVICTIONS

Perhaps your tenant's behavior has so aggravated you that you decide to take matters into your own hands by changing the locks on the doors or by physically removing your tenant's furniture and having it stored in your garage. What you risk is not only harsh legal repercussions—the certainty of criminal and perhaps civil penalties—but also your tenant's wrath and retaliation. Your tenant could turn around and take action against you, both legally and physically. Although taking the proper steps to evict your tenant properly through the appropriate channels may seem endless, frustrating and maddening, it will probably give you the result you want—possession of your apartment. In short, don't try "self-help."

What about offering your tenant a cash payment to move? Some landlords swear by this method and claim the cash acts as an incentive to get the tenant out quickly. This method may work when your tenant is being evicted because of changing economic circumstances—let's say two men lived in your apartment and one of them moved out. The one left behind couldn't find a roommate and got behind in his rent. He claims he is looking for a smaller, more economical apartment but cannot come up with the advance money. If it looks as though the eviction process could take longer than a month, then it might make some sense to give your tenant the money to get himself out. This, however, is only recommended in the most unusual circumstances. Your offer to "buy the tenant out" could be used against you in court; your tenant could take it as a form of harassment or intimidation.

SUMMARY PROCESS

So, you've tried everything. You've given Jim Tenant chances, you've given him legal notice, and you're still stuck with him. Up to this point, your relationship has been a two-party one, between you and your tenant. Now a third party, the court, enters the relationship. When the time specified in your Notice to Quit has lapsed and your tenant has not paid the rent, corrected the violations, or moved, then you must file a formal complaint in court. Go down to the courthouse. Usually this is done in the housing court, but call in advance to be sure.

At the courthouse, you will fill out a standard complaint form which names the tenant, the apartment number and the reason(s) for the eviction proceedings. Depending on the circumstances, your reason would be "Nonpayment of rent" or "Violation of Clause 3 of the lease," for example. The form will summon you and your tenant to a hearing anywhere from seven to thirty days later, depending on the laws in your area. This formal complaint is then served on the tenant by the court; you are responsible for paying for the service and often also for a "filing fee," both of which are nominal charges. It's a good idea to bring along a copy of your rental agreement or lease.

Within a specified period of time, your tenant then will have the opportunity to file an "Answer" to your complaint, denying your charges of failure to pay rent, claiming notice was never or improperly served, and the like. His answer is his defense against your attempts to evict him. Your tenant may file for "Discovery," a tactic by which he can legally request certain information and documents, including your receipts, lease agreement and rent receipts. These are in addition to any counterclaims your tenant makes against you. In general, these tactics are used as delay tactics but may form the basis for a judge to find you at fault and award your tenant damages. If your tenant files an answer, then the hearing date is postponed by a specified length of time, depending on your area.

When the hearing date finally arrives, you will go to the courthouse and present your side of the story. Bring with you documents, records, receipts, photographs, bounced checks, letters to or from your tenant, a copy of your lease or rental agreement, a copy of the Apartment Condition Report, and photographs of damage. Ask any witnesses to accompany you, including repairmen who fixed damage (but be prepared to pay them for their time). Your tenant will also have the opportunity to present his side of the story. Because your blood may begin to boil in the courtroom, it is wise to rehearse exactly what you plan to say and even write out the facts and dates you consider important. These will help you be objective before the judge and keep your mind on the issues at hand.

The judge will probably grant the eviction, but you may not "win" in the traditional expected sense. For example, your tenant may claim hardship and be granted a "stay," by which he is allowed to stay in the apartment for, say, six months while he finds a new apartment for himself and his family. Your tenant may also appeal the judgment or not be forced to pay back rent.

Once the judge has ruled that the tenant vacate the premises, you may have the legal right to hire movers and remove and store the tenant's possessions. (Most tenants will have, by this time, moved themselves.) If you have not hired an attorney before this point, you definitely should consult one before taking this drastic but necessary step. Take heart, though: this is a relatively uncommon occurrence.

One of the best feelings in the whole world is to open the door of the empty apartment of an evicted tenant. Short of opening a bottle of champagne over the mantel, you'll want to celebrate having the apartment back in your possession. After you close the door on that tenant, you'll want to look around, count the bedrooms, assess the condition, define the space, decide the rent, place an ad and . . .

Suggestions for Further Reading

No landlord's bookshelf should lack the local housing code and rent regulations and the free U.S. government publications "Rental Property," "Depreciation," "Business Use of Your Home," and "Wise Rental Practices." The following books are also useful.

Allen, Robert G., *Nothing Down* (Simon & Schuster, New York, 1980).

Bierbrier, Doreen, *Living with Tenants* (The Housing Connection, Arlington, Virginia, 1983).

Legal Tactics: A Handbook for Massachusetts Tenants (Cambridge Tenants Organization, Cambridge, 1980).

Lapatin, Philip S., and Herbert S. Lerman, *Residential Landlord-Tenant Law: A Modern Massachusetts Guide,* 2nd ed. (Rental Housing Association, Boston, 1982).

Lowry, Albert J., *How You Can Become Financially Independent by Investing in Real Estate* (Simon & Schuster, New York, 1982).

Lowry, Albert J., *How to Manage Real Estate Successfully—in Your Spare Time* (Simon & Schuster, New York, 1977).

Nessen, Robert L., *The Real Estate Book* (Little, Brown and Company, Boston, 1981).

Robinson, Leigh, *Landlording: A Handy Manual for Scrupulous Landlords and Landladies Who Do It Themselves,* 3rd ed. (Express, Richmond, California, 1981).

Striker, John M., and Andrew O. Shapiro, *Super Tenant: New York City Tenant Handbook,* 2nd ed. (Holt, Rinehart and Winston, New York, 1978).

Acknowledgments

We are grateful to the many landlords who shared their experiences with us, especially to Steve and Nancy Bowen, David Campbell, Meredith and Larry Delamarter, Henry Horenstein, Nan Jernigan, Peter and Carol Judge, Michael Owens, Jack Marr and Glen Steer.

Also, to Nina Groskind for her enthusiasm for the project.

To our families, for their support.

To our friends who have asked us over the years what it is like to be a landlord: we appreciate your many questions and particularly thank Christina Coffin, Christina Ward and George Ward.

A special note of thanks goes to Caroline Patterson, without whom there would have been no typed manuscript; her unflagging optimism, helpful suggestions and zest for the project inspired us.

To Jim Fitzgerald and Casey Fuetsch, our editors at Doubleday, for their patience.

Finally, we will always be grateful to Carol Mann, our agent, for her faith in us.

Index